FOCUSED
(on their future),

FEARLESS
(of the consequences), and

FIGHTING
(for their lives)

A Raw and Uncut Guide to
Raising Productive, Ambitious Children

Nicole Petite

FOCUSED (on their future), FEARLESS (of the consequences), and FIGHTING (for their lives): A Raw and Uncut Guide to Raising Productive, Ambitious Children

Copyright © 2017 by Nicole Petite
Revised 2024

Edited by Candace Johnson

All rights reserved. No part of this book may be reproduced or transmitted in any form or by any means without written permission of the author.

By no means do I claim to be a perfect parent or adult. My views and experiences referenced in this book are a reflection as to what has worked for me to help raise my girls as well as change the perspective of life with other children I meet. My role as an adult and a parent is to always assist and improve the lives of any child because of the experiences I have had growing up. This book only relates to my opinions and some research from selected resources and I always suggest that a reader check for other resources as well.

ISBN 978-0-692-98704-9

Dedication

As I type this, I shake and cry because I am still in disbelief this life changing event has taken place so unexpectedly. I am dedicating this book to a very special woman in my life, Nana. A woman that has helped raise me for 22 years of my life. I will forever be indebted to you. I mourn your absence but try hard to celebrate your life and being honored to have been a part of it for so long. You were and will always be one of a kind. You made sure everyone stuck together as a family and you always told all of us to, "Do what's right. No matter how it makes you feel." I will always keep that in mind when making decisions throughout the rest of my life. May your husband, three boys, and grandchildren continue to speak life into your spirit and allow your memories to live among us all. Nana, I love you with all of my heart and soul and always will. I will never, ever forget you. EVER.

Parental Control

How many of you are willing to face the reality
that raising independent strong minds
is not within your capability?

Would you feel like a failure if you realized
that your way of parenting was wrong?
That it is your obligation to control what they are exposed
to whether televised, schooled, or even in a simple song?

Parentally you are able to choose between
hands-on versus hands tied,
and not be at the mercy of mistakes in this journey,
but have an authentic, step-by-step guide.

Take this journey, if you will, of parental
enlightenment, and choose focus and clarity,
while discovering freedom from follower's
mindsets and embracing your authority.

Parental friendship over guidance and discipline
lacks fortitude and a strong foundation,
redirect from that path, hone your perception, and
take step one toward your child's emancipation.

Angela Agnew

Contents

Introduction 1
1 Conception and Pregnancy 9
2 No Longer Alone 37
3 Preschool Years (Ages 3 to 5). 63
4 Grammar School (Ages 6 to 10) 77
5 Middle School (Preteen Years) 101

How's Your Mental? 137

6 High School (Teen Years). 143
7 College and Beyond. 163
References. 169

Introduction

If you have a child or children, or plan on having any children, this book is for you. If you've ever had a five-minute conversation with any child, this book is for you. *Focused, Fearless, and Fighting* is based on my own experiences raising two girls and uplifting and changing the mindset of the boys and girls around me on a variety of subjects, including self-esteem building, sex and self-respect, history, bullying, education, and career choices.

Nice to Meet You. Let's Get Started.

I work every day to convince young people to keep striving to be the best they can be, even when they have no one to listen to them or support them. Through my organization and public speaking, I also provide resources to students, young adults, and parents to better position themselves to succeed in life. It takes a strong and focused individual, man or woman, to raise a child to be career-oriented, independent, and driven. Instilling these three characteristics is essential to having a peace of mind that your child will be okay and a sense of pride as a parent that your child can hold his or her own in this brutal world. Leaders are not born. They are raised. And you are raising them.

By no means do I claim to be the world's best mom or the parent who knows everything there is to know about raising children. What I do know is that my teachings will give my daughters the tools to be successful in life after I am long gone, and if they choose anything different from what they were taught, their choices will not be made out of ignorance. They have been given the knowledge and resources to succeed and make great choices in life, and it's up to them to make the most of it all.

As I write this book, my older daughter is a junior in college, and she has maintained a 3.7 GPA while majoring in biology/pre-med. She finished her last sophomore semester with a 4.0 GPA. My younger daughter is currently in the tenth grade. She finished her freshman year with a 3.7 also. Her plan was to finish her last quarter with a 4.0. Her biggest influence and competition is her sister. They made a challenge that if both made a 4.0 at the end of the year, they would both have to treat each other to dinner. If only one completed the challenge, the other would have to take the winner to dinner. I

How you treat your child is how she will treat others. Hurt people hurt people, and loved people show love.

ended up taking both to dinner to celebrate them both. My youngest checks her grades every day to stay on top of what she needs to do to meet my expectations and to succeed in reaching her own goals. She's on the A/B honor roll and on track for college. As of 2024, my older daughter is in her 4th year of medical school and my youngest just graduated with her undergraduate degree in Computer Science with a concentration in Cybersecurity, Cum Laude.

My two daughters are like night and day, but my younger wants to mimic her older sister. I have always said that I think my younger daughter stands over her sister and watches her sleep in order to pick up some of her characteristics and absorb her traits. Seriously.

My mom has never been one to sugarcoat communication with me, and I think my mom did a great job with me, so my girls get the exact same treatment. So far, so good.

Throughout this book, I'll push you to be straight up with your child on every subject too. Sugarcoating things will only handicap him. I also forbid my daughters to use the word "can't" in my home or presence. That was literally a curse word in my home. They still remember that and refuse to say that word, or they find themselves correcting themselves midsentence if they start to say it.

My commitment to helping our children succeed extends to the community, and I currently co-host a club for youth and adults called The Six Figure Club. Through this organization, I, alongside with a partner, expose students and adults to a wide variety of six-figure careers, some of which they might not otherwise know about or consider pursuing. We have been told all of our lives to become a doctor or a lawyer to build wealth, but that gives our children false hope. We know not everyone will become a doctor or a lawyer, but there are so many other careers out there that gross six figures annually. The purpose of finding a six-figure career is to begin to build wealth for themselves and their families. Introducing our children to careers in which they can build wealth and possibly start their own businesses gives them opportunities to change their lives and the lives of their loved ones that they otherwise would not have.

I also had a program called Takingovermyfuture.com. It was a web-based program through which I assisted students with preparing for post-educational success in college, trade school, the military, or the workforce. I helped them find scholarships, advised them about what to do when they reach a certain grade level, and directed them to the resources to get it done. So far, every senior who participated in the program is in college and headed towards graduation. I also speak in schools, church groups, and conferences to students and adults about education, life obstacles, and how to conquer them.

It has been said that a child comes without instructions. In today's society, we all need reliable resources to lead us in the right direction. I am sharing my own path in this book. Even though I have two girls, the manner that I chose to raise them will work for both boys and girls. Children are children. They will be who they are. The character you help them mold will shape their future. Responsible adults need to realize that we too are only human. We will make mistakes as parents. How we handle our mistakes and correct them is up to us. That's what will make a difference for our children.

The end goal of raising children is to make sure they are prepared for the real world, whatever that means to you as a parent. So open your heart and your mind and try to be receptive to the guidance in this book. Some of my philosophies have been, and still are, a little unorthodox, but we are raising children in an unorthodox environment and time, so we must adapt to life. Life will not adapt to us.

My Upbringing

It was easier for me than it may have been for many other mothers to determine how I wanted to raise my daughters because I could just mimic the way my mother raised my brother and me. I was born to an African American mother and father with my strongest support coming from my mother. She was a single mother, for the most part, and was very good at it. In fact, I didn't notice how good she was at it until I became an adult myself. She never bashed my biological dad for not being there. His absence was something we saw for ourselves. My mother didn't give me many limitations as I grew up, either. She saved those until I got older. At that point, she gave me an earlier curfew. It wasn't until I was an adult that I realized that she wanted me home during late hours because of what I could be engaging in, like sex. Slick woman! Luckily, I wasn't engaging in sexual intercourse at such a young age. I wasn't developed physically, so that may have saved me. No one noticed me in those days. It is a lot different for many young girls growing up today. Their bodies are developing faster than their brains. That's dangerous.

My mother also never tried to raise my brother to be a man. She raised him to be a responsible adult. He did have a few male role models to look up to, one of whom was the man we both decided to call "Dad." I was three years old when he entered my life and repaired everything around me. Literally. When he came into our lives, almost everything that needed repairing in the house had been duct-taped together. That was what my biological father did when things broke down. Fortunately, Dad taught us that was not the way to fix things. He came in and replaced it all. That was the first time I saw the actions of a real man, and it didn't stop there. It came natural for Dad to do those things for my mom. They never married, but he was there for her and us. Weird, huh? I know, but it worked. As I write this book, he still calls me his baby girl and makes sure I have everything I need. When I first met Dad, I hated him. I am so glad I gave him a chance.

My mother taught me to be independent but to also be a lady. Even though she and Dad did not marry, her plan was for me to marry one day but also be able to take care of myself, and even take care of my husband if he ever needed me to. She instilled those values in me from my early childhood, and when it was time for me to graduate from high school, she advised me that either I could go to college or I could die. As a young teen, that was scary, and she articulated those words with force and conviction on a regular basis. Back in those days, we didn't have social media and other distractions, so I had only her to listen to, which turned out to be great for me.

How you treat and react to your child plays a major role in how his character develops.

One of my cousins who I was close to attended college, so I did have a little knowledge of why my mom stressed higher education. This cousin was one of my role models. She went to college and graduated, and her success let me know graduating was in my reach. That was my motivation to not only attend college, but to finish with my degree. My cousin took me almost everywhere with her, including some places I probably should not have been, but her teachings were always positive. I was only an observer in her world, and she always made sure I was okay.

My mom trusted her as well. Her trust was very important because she wouldn't leave us with just anyone. Only a select few adults were allowed to supervise us. If no one she trusted was available, my mom would not go wherever it was she wanted to go. If someone she didn't trust wanted to be left alone with us, her answer was always no. No exceptions. She never compromised our safety to go out or to make us happy.

My mom spent time with my brother and me. She told us she loved us, and we were able to ask her grown-up questions. Some she answered, and some she felt we couldn't handle the answer to, in which case she would advise us that we were too young to know the answer at that moment. If social media was around back then, I am sure she would have answered every question we asked at the time we asked. Occasionally, she told us the answers were none of our business, but she *never* made us feel as if any question was off limits.

The way my mother raised me heavily influenced me to write this book. My mom ruled with an iron fist, but she was also a woman who loved her children, and she showed us that love every day. Her parenting skills came from a place of truth, love, and discipline. I must say it worked. She loved us, fussed at us, spanked us, hugged us, kissed us, and told us she loved us. We saw her sacrifice for us on a daily basis. We didn't have much, but we didn't know how little we had because she made sure we never went without.

My promise to you and all who read this book is that you will find something in *Focused, Fearless, and Fighting* that you can use to increase your child's chances of success in life right away. Of course I would recommend that you read this book in its entirety, but you can also jump to different chapters as needed. If you are just getting this book and you have a middle-school child or high school child, go ahead and dive into those chapters to get some pointers for those life stages. Once you have gained some insight for what can be done immediately for the child you have at home, start from the beginning. In all likelihood, you know someone who can use this information, or you can see what you could have done better and start to work on your flaws. (No stress.

We all have them.) Wherever you start, read the entire book. You bought it, so you might as well get your money's worth.

LESSON 1
Conception and Pregnancy

Let's talk about sex.

As adults, most of us have encountered or will encounter that intimate moment when we have the potential to create a child. Before engaging in sex, we must force ourselves to think with our brains and not with our bodies and hearts. We must understand that condoms are only 82 percent effective and women can still become pregnant, and either partner can still contract an STD[1] even when condoms are used. Given those facts, we have to be mindful of who we decide to engage in these sexual acts with.

As a woman, you have to ask yourself, "If I were to become pregnant, would he be a great father?" Yes, *great*. What is a great father? It depends on who you ask. A great father, to me, is someone who nurtures his child, a man who provides for his household and expresses the love he has for his child while showing that child how to be loved by showing that love to the mother of his child whether they are

---

[1] Planned Parenthood. (2016, March 10). How effective are condoms? Retrieved March 02, 2017, from [https://www.plannedparenthood.org/learn/birth-control/condom/how-effective-are-condoms

together or not. That will be the first love that a child sees, how a father treats the mother of his children. What she sees determines how she feels about you as a father and will help her choose the man of her dreams whether a repeat of how you mistreat and disrespect her mother OR she will make sure her husband is NOTHING like the father because of the hurt she has seen her mother go through which hurts her as well. If he is providing an environment and rules that will allow the child to love and be successful, then he is a great father. A good father no longer is good enough. He must be an active father in order to make a positive difference in a world filled with distractions.

You also need to know if he already has other children. If so, is he a father to them? Alternatively, can he be a father to the other child(ren)? Is the mother bitter toward your potential baby's father? Does she still want to be with him? Financially, can he afford to have any more children? Is he responsible? Does he have children and abandon them? Was the mother he had the baby with someone he had a long-term relationship with or a one-night stand? These questions should definitely be clarified before you climb in bed with him and risk making him a father again. You don't have to give him the third degree to find out these answers. The answers will show themselves, unless he's a one-night stand and you don't have time to get to know him. (And yes, men need to ask themselves the same things about any woman they intend to have sex with because not every woman will be a *great* mother either.)

Is your potential sex partner bisexual? This question is important because if the man is having sex with both men and women, he can put the woman at greater risk for sexually transmitted disease. It has been proven that having anal sex increases the chances of contracting sexually transmitted diseases. This includes an increased risk of hepatitis, HIV/AIDS, and herpes[2]. Straight, gay, or bisexual, you need to consider whether or not he might carry any diseases that have not surfaced or may never surface until it's too late. Many of these diseases can affect your unborn child if you become pregnant, and they would certainly affect you.

These are essential questions you must ask yourself every time you decide to have sex. Either party can be irresponsible. As dramatic as it may sound, we should all relate to our sexual partners as potential co-parents. Men and women, girls and boys should honor their bodies in that fashion. Be selective.

It would be great if all of us were so selective all the time. Well, a girl can dream, right? As I've taught my daughters, if you are not prepared for the consequences, you should not engage in any sexual activity. If you are not comfortable enough to engage in a sexual activity with the lights on and grab the penis with your hand, stare the penis in its face, and examine it, don't put it in you. (I'm sure you had a visual. Good! It's that important.) Those few moments can alter your life for the worse.

---

2 CDC Fact Sheet: What Gay, Bisexual and Other Men Who Have Sex with Men Need to Know About Sexually Transmitted Diseases. (2016, October 18). Retrieved March 02, 2017, from https://www.cdc.gov/std/life-stages-populations/stdfact-msm.htm

Of course, just looking at a penis (or vagina) won't tell you if your partner has an STD, but it is an extra precaution and gives you time to think about whether or not you really want to move forward. The best thing to do beforehand is, in a setting that isn't likely to lead to sex, talk about the possible consequences with your potential partner. A phone conversation will work because you won't be tempted to jump right in just because the answers are what you want to hear.

If he's willing to have that conversation, that is great news! If he evades the conversation, that response should make your radar go off. He may be uncomfortable, but that may also mean he has never been tested. It could mean a lot of things. He should never be a candidate for sex. If you avoid him and eliminate anyone who will not have the discussion with you, you lessen your chances of becoming pregnant or getting an STD. You will be surprised at the number of men and women who do not want to have a conversation about STDs. So talk about it up front and long before the encounter.

I also advise young men that they should ask any young lady who they are about to or planning to have a sexual encounter with if she knows what a Pap smear is and if she's ever had one. If her answer is no, and this is not her first sexual encounter, he should get up, pull his pants up, and never look back. Any female engaging in sexual activity should be receiving a regular checkup, focused on her genitals, once a year. If she is not, how can she tell her partner what's going on down there? She doesn't know herself. That's one less baby mama a young man will have to worry about.

Many parents are forced to be parents simply because of a night of good, or not so good, sex. When you become a parent as a result of these one-night stands or short-term relationships, you are forced to become something you didn't plan to be. You may have an unstable financial circumstance, an unprepared mental state, or just suffer from plain immaturity, but if you are not ready, you will deal with consequences when the child is born.

There are times when a woman and a man will recognize they need to change and prepare themselves during pregnancy to become a mother and a father and be the best parents they can be. However, this isn't always the case. Some parents who conceive children unexpectedly or who regret being pregnant resent that child when he or she is born. They feel as if the child has negatively changed their lives in a way they never intended, even though the child didn't ask to be here and had absolutely nothing to do with the parents engaging in the sexual activity that caused the child to exist in the first place.

Once we, as adults, can learn to accept the outcomes when engaging in sex, our choice to conceive will be welcomed and not considered a burden. Let me ask you an important question. Are you sure you're ready for a baby? If the answer is yes, keep on reading! If the answer is no and you are already pregnant, keep on reading! And more importantly, if the baby is already here and you are confused or overwhelmed and resentful, take a really deep breath, send the child off to a responsible adult you trust, grab a glass of wine to relax (if you are of legal age), and keep reading! You just may have a change of heart!

Choosing a Co-Parent

> *How in the world did this guy end up on top of me?*
> *What was I thinking?*
> *What did I see in him?*

If you are in the position to be thinking any of those things, it's a little too late to ask those questions and, more importantly, too late to determine if he will be a good or great father or not. Knowing you have a chance to become pregnant every time you have a sexual encounter should reduce your chances of lying horizontally with the wrong person. Was he cute (in the eye of the beholder)? Did he have on fancy clothes and jewelry? Did he give you attention that you weren't used to getting? Maybe you were looking for acceptance from a man because you had no father in your home, or a man mistreated you when you were growing up or when you were in a previous relationship. Maybe you've never learned your real worth.

All of those factors, as well as others not mentioned, play a role in your choice of men. Similar factors influence how a man chooses women, including things like whether or not she resembles his mother, her physical attributes, and how she makes him feel about himself. None of these characteristics give you a clue about whether or not that partner would be a good or great parent. In making these choices, we tend to think with our vaginas and penises and not our brains. When we use body parts to think with, parts that are not programmed for thinking, we always mess up. This is why it is very important to have the discussion about sex before we get to the act and when the environment is not sexually enticing.

I believe in striving for a family with both parents in the same home. I'm not against single-family homes, but no man should make a woman a mother if she is not worth being made a wife. And no woman should make a man a father if he is not yet learned to be a husband. The list below will give you a great start on what to ask yourself or your potential partner before you enter a sexual relationship:

For Him

- ✔ What is her HIV/STD status?
- ✔ Does she have any children?
- ✔ Does she take good care of those children?
- ✔ If so, does she get along with the baby's father?
- ✔ Are they still dating or seeing each other sexually?
- ✔ Does she take care of her health? Does she see her doctor annually?
- ✔ Has she had any cosmetic surgery? You think your child will look like you and her, but because of cosmetic surgery to reshape a weirdly shaped nose, big lips, funny-looking ears, or other physical attributes,

the baby could end up looking like someone you have never seen before.
- ✔ Is she financially stable?
- ✔ Does she have any mental health issues?
- ✔ Does her family have a history of health issues, either physical or mental?
- ✔ Can she have children?

For Her

- ✔ What is his STD/HIV status?
- ✔ Does he have any children?
- ✔ If so, does he get along with the baby's mother?
- ✔ If he has any children, is he involved in their lives?
- ✔ Are he and the mother still dating or seeing each other sexually?
- ✔ Does he consider himself bisexual, or is he unsure about his sexuality?
- ✔ Does he take care of his health? Does he see his doctor annually?
- ✔ Is he financially stable?
- ✔ Does he have any mental health issues?
- ✔ Does his family have a history of health issues, either physical or mental?
- ✔ Can he have children?

Pregnancy

Planned or not, it happened. Now, you are growing a life in your body. How incredible is that? And to have a healthy child is even more amazing! Are you excited about having a child, or are you excited about raising a child? There is a major difference between the two. For some young parents, having a child is just a fad or something cute to do, while for others it seems like the end of the world. In 2014, there were 24.2 births for every 1,000 adolescent females ages fifteen to nineteen, or 249,078 babies born to females in this age group. Nearly 89 percent of these births occurred outside of marriage. [3]

The 2014 teen birth rate indicates a decline of 9 percent from 2013, when the birth rate was 26.5 per 1,000. The teen birth rate has declined almost continuously over the past twenty years. In 1991, the U.S. teen birth rate was 61.8 births for every 1,000 adolescent females, compared with 24.2 births for every 1,000 adolescent females in 2014. Still, the U.S. teen birth rate is higher than that of many other developed countries, including Canada and the United Kingdom.[4] Not all mothers, of course, are teenagers having babies; many are true adults. But the concept is the same. They are okay with being pregnant but not yet ready to take on raising a baby.

---

[3] The Office of Adolescent Health, U.S. Department of Health and Human Services." Office of Adolescent Health. N.p., 27 Feb. 2016. Web. 27 Feb. 2016. <http://www.hhs.gov/ash/oah/adolescent-health-topics/reproductive-health/teen-pregnancy/trends.html#>.

[4] Pregnant Teen Mannequins at the Mall Are Sending a Mixed Message. (2014, November 13). Retrieved March 02, 2017, from https://www.yahoo.com/style/pregnant-teen-mannequins-at-the-mall-are-sending-a-102547296423.html

So herein lies the problem. Some of these adolescent (or just young) mothers also had adolescent mothers. Some were girls who were neglected by their own parents, and the daughters were repeating the cycle. And guess where the pregnant teen's mother and father were when she made a decision to become sexually active and failed to use adequate protection? Many of these grandparents-to-be were out sowing their royal oats because they'd had children prematurely and felt like they'd missed out on their own youth. They were focused on making up for lost time.

Of course, teenage pregnancy isn't always the result of a family legacy or of parental neglect, and some young parents will step up to fulfill their obligations to their children and each other. Unfortunately, babies don't get to choose to be born to the exceptional young parents. All too many are born to adults who want to have a baby, even though they have no idea what that will mean for their lives or the baby's life in the short term or over the long run. Worse than that, they may repeat the abuse or neglect they've suffered, not realizing how much harm was done to them.

Many parents never think through a plan to raise the baby. They just want to have the baby. This type of decision-making is often the result of neglected girls looking for love in all the wrong places. They're looking to prove their worth in the streets or with a male figure, neither of which is healthy for them. The end result of that decision-making is a family of degenerates—children and adults with no standards for education, no ability to take care of themselves or any children they may have of their own, and a lifetime spent simply trying to survive in this cruel world. They have bought in to "survival of the fittest" because they have to. They struggle to eat; they have no guidance and are left in this world to fend for themselves the best way they know how. That leads to crime.

Raising a child is much different from giving birth or the fantasy of being a parent. What you do with your mind, body, and spirit from conception on impacts the life you will give birth to in thirty-six to forty weeks (assuming you carry to full term). Pregnancy gives the mother and the father the time to prepare for the upbringing of this child. Together, the mother and father can decide if the environment is safe for the new baby or if it is hazardous for the child to be in. The parents can determine if the environment is child friendly or if they both need to move out of the area to protect the child's physical, mental, or emotional wellbeing. That's a lot to think about, huh? Yes, it is. But remember, you knew this could happen before you did the "grown folks," right? Even if you didn't plan to be a parent, there is still hope.

Now, if you decide that raising a baby is not for you, and you give birth to the child, I always recommend giving that bundle of joy to someone who cannot conceive on their own or who wishes to raise a child who needs a home. Adoption is a kinder choice than raising a baby you will resent. There are options from completely closed adoptions, where your name is never revealed, to open adoptions, where all the involved parents can decide how much of a relationship they want to maintain. It's a good option for some women.

Of course, my goal with this book is to guide you to love and raise the child as your own if possible.

Connecting with Your Child

During each of my pregnancies, I sang to my girls and rubbed my tummy all the time. I did this in hopes that they would recognize my voice when

If you are calling your child a bitch, slut, whore, nigga, bastard, lil fucka, cunt, stupid, ugly, bitch ass nigga, all through his or her life you are the problem. What you call your children is what they will become.

they were born. I think it worked! When each one was born, her reaction to my voice was incredible and could be easily defined as voice recognition. This is the first connection babies have with their parents.

After my daughters were born, I always spoke softly to them, never raising my voice, always gentle. When speaking to children, your tone and how you speak have a real impact on them, and they will learn whatever tone you speak, and mimic that in life. For example, my brother is a Marine veteran, and because of his military experiences he is always loud. Just loud for no reason at all. He doesn't know the definition of whispering. Well, he had an offspring. Guess what. Yes! She is loud too! For no apparent reason at all. Actually, in her case, it can sometimes be cute and funny because I know it is simply a learned behavior. My brother is a single father, so his daughter really doesn't have anyone else to mimic as closely as her father. My mom is also in the home with them, and you'd better believe that my niece has picked up some of my mom's habits good, bad, or neutral too.

In essence, you have to be mindful of all you do because the child will learn it, whether you want him to or not. A child will hear what you say but listen to what you do. I say that a lot because I know it to be true: your influence on your child's behavior and choices is rarely about what you say but mostly what you do, how you behave, and how you live your life.

I became a mother the moment I found out I was pregnant. That was my chosen mindset. Yes, it is a choice. During my pregnancies, I made sure I took my prescribed prenatal vitamins. I wanted to give birth to the healthiest baby I could. There are several illnesses that can be prevented based on how well you take the proper vitamins. For example, according to Bay Center Medical Advisory Board, folic acid helps prevent neural tube defects (NTDs)—serious birth defects of the spinal cord (such as spina bifida) and the brain (such as anencephaly). Neural tube defects occur at a very early stage of development, before many women even know they're pregnant. They affect about 3,000 pregnancies a year in the United States. [5] It's important that you talk to your doctor,

---

5   Folic acid: Why you need it before and during pregnancy | BabyCenter. (2013, March). Retrieved March 21, 2016, from http://www.babycenter. com/0_folic-acid-why-you-need-it-before-and-during-pregnancy_476.bc

find out what supplements to take during your pregnancy, and take them as prescribed.

During my pregnancy, I also made sure I wasn't hanging out in smoke-filled places, places filled with loud music, or rowdy environments. I always felt as if, even in the first trimester, my babies knew when I was somewhere I should not have been, and they would punish me for it somehow, probably with the dreaded morning sickness. Choose your environment carefully throughout your pregnancy and avoid any place that could be physically or mentally toxic to you and your unborn baby.

Make sure you see and consult with your doctor on a regular basis. Keep your doctor appointments throughout your pregnancy. If there is ever a time when you are unable to make a scheduled appointment, reschedule immediately. Your doctor will monitor your health, the baby's growth, and other factors to look out for any potential problems. That can only happen if you show up for regular examinations and testing. If you discover anything that seems unusual to you, contact your doctor immediately.

Selfless—the New You

During pregnancy you have to determine if you have been selfless throughout your life or if this is something you need to learn to be. Take a good look at yourself and how you've lived your life so far, and decide if this is an area you need to work on. If so, get started right away. Selflessness is one major aspect of a parent's life because there is a lot of truth to the saying that your life ends when your child is born. A more accurate observation is that your life is and should be altered to focus on someone who has no idea at all what this world will offer her. Your child's first experience of the world comes from you. Being selfless means you build your entire life around raising this child. Sound depressing? Let me rephrase that. You are now responsible for the life or death of your child and your child's future. What are you going to do with that responsibility? Let me try one more time. This new baby thinks you are the world, so whatever is in your world, you will directly or indirectly introduce to this child. Okay, that may not be a refreshing thought either, but you get the point. I will not attempt to sugarcoat something so important.

You have to face your fears immediately and not try to avoid what is to come. Avoiding it is like avoiding cancer. It won't go away; it will only get worse if it goes untreated. It's always better to develop that characteristic of selflessness before you become a parent, but if you haven't, you need to do it now.

Selflessness means being concerned more with the needs of others than with your own and putting someone else's needs before your own. Those types of environments, where no one will look out for you and your baby when you need them, will have a negative impact on you and your child. Remember that a lot of your child's behaviors will be learned, whether you want them to be or not. Stay away as much as possible from people who aren't positive influences. If a close family member, let's just say your mom, is demonstrating bad behavior, make sure you talk to your child as he gets older and explain that your mom is wrong, especially if her actions are negatively affecting your child. Of course, in some form of communication, inform your mom you are not happy with a certain behavior in front of your child. It will be hard to stop allowing your child to be around your mom, but it's unlikely that your mom will change. There is no other way to express that. But hey, she just might change for her grandbabies if she didn't change for you. If she doesn't, the children need to know that certain behaviors are not okay, and they need you to tell them emphatically that the behavior is unacceptable. The child needs to know you mean what you say and say what you mean. And if it comes down to it, you may have to set boundaries that severely limit or eliminate the time your child spends with this person with or without you there to serve as a buffer.

The next thing you need to do is eliminate habits in your life that would upset you if you found out your child were doing the exact same thing. It will be easier to make improvements if you start breaking bad habits while you're pregnant especially since you know the doctor is watching. (Remember that regular prenatal visits are a must.) Bad habits, such as using drugs, drinking, smoking cigarettes, the use of profanity, and other destructive behaviors should come to mind as you check yourself for necessary changes.

While we are on the subject of profanity, allow me to elaborate. One of the worst things you can do as a parent is demean your child by calling him or her bad names. Calling them names that include curse words is even more hurtful, and this is true even while that child is still growing in your womb. Your emotions affect you physically, and they affect the child growing in your body. If you develop this bad habit while you're pregnant, it will be hard to break once the child is born. If you use profanity when you address your child, she will pick up on that and start to use those exact words towards everyone else, and may eventually use them on you. You will also create a child whose self-worth and self-respect are destroyed by your verbal abuse.

I have a question for you. Do you smoke cigarettes? This is a sensitive topic for me because my mom smoked when I was growing up in her house. I actually loved the smell of her lighting up a cigarette, but let me get back to the topic at hand (I was having a nostalgic moment). If you are a smoker and you are expecting, you must stop. Smoking cigarettes is one of the worst things you can do to an unborn child (and to a born child). Cigarette smoke contains more than 4,000 chemicals, including truly nasty things like cyanide, lead, and at least sixty cancer-causing compounds. When you smoke during pregnancy, that toxic brew gets into your bloodstream, your baby's only source of oxygen and nutrients. As for smoking after the child is born, millions of children are breathing in secondhand smoke in their own homes[6]. Secondhand smoke can be especially harmful to your

---

6   The Dangers of Secondhand Smoke. (n.d.). Retrieved March 02, 2017, from https://www.healthychildren.org/English/health-issues/conditions/tobacco/Pages/Dangers-of-Secondhand-Smoke.aspx

children's health because their lungs still are developing. If you smoke, the best thing you can do for your child, and for yourself, is to stop now. Not slow down, or smoke when the baby is not around, but completely stop.

It should go without saying that using drugs during your pregnancy could have severe consequences for your child, but I'm going to say it so there's no confusion. If you're using any kinds of drugs while you're pregnant, get whatever help you need to stop. This includes marijuana, prescription drugs taken inappropriately, and any illegal drugs. Children born to mothers who abuse substances like these suffer through withdrawals in the early days of their lives, and it's hard to watch. The long-term consequences they may suffer are unpredictable and can be life-altering for the negative. Your high is not worth the risk to your child. If you can't stop on your own, find help. Now.

Alcohol may be a legal substance, but it's one of the most dangerous for an unborn child. Fetal alcohol syndrome can leave a child with facial deformities, lower IQ, growth problems, and even mental retardation.[7] If you drank before you knew you were pregnant, what's done is done, but you now have no excuse to continue to expose your child to this danger. If you can't stop drinking, you have an addiction, and you need to acknowledge that and get help immediately.

---

7 Harding, D. M. (n.d.). Fetal Alcohol Syndrome. Alcohol in pregnancy and effects. Retrieved March 08, 2017, from http://patient.info/health/fetal-alcohol-syndrome-leaflet

When you choose to be selfless and put your child's well-being ahead of your desire to hang out and have fun or your habit of reducing your pain and coping with problems by using substances, you choose to start on your way to becoming a great parent. Your child is worth it.

What one or two people in this world you would drop everything and do anything for? We all have at least one person we are willing to do anything for. Who is it for you now? If you have at least one person, that's great news! That means you already know how to be selfless. The bad news is that you must figure out how to replace that person with your child and make sure your child is on the list of people that you'd "do anything for."

During pregnancy, a relationship should start to grow between you and your unborn child. You can help build this relationship by giving the child a name early in your pregnancy and calling that child by his or her name instead of "it" or "the baby." When you identify with the child as a human being, it's easier to become attached to the baby, which is a good thing.

Let young men be boys. Don't force them to learn manly activities before their time.

Establishing a relationship with your baby while he or she is still in your tummy is an important part of becoming selfless. Talk to him, sing to her, and pay attention to your son or daughter's growth. Share the ultrasound pictures with family and friends. (If they don't care, share them on social media, and someone will like your pictures.) All of these things will allow you to fall in love with your baby before he or she gets here, and love usually begets selflessness.

Self-Care

While you're making good decisions for the health of your baby, don't forget that includes taking care of yourself. Make sure you get enough rest, and ask for help when you need it. If help is not available, slow down. Confide in someone who has your best interest at heart. It's okay to tell someone you need help. We all do at different times. Get the amount of exercise your doctor recommends for you, and eat plenty of fruits and vegetables or at least the healthiest foods you can tolerate and enjoy. Minimize the junk food you eat, and minimize the stress in your life. Maybe try some meditating. It may work for you, if done properly. It may not. It helps if you don't put pressure on yourself to get it right.

Stay out of other people's drama, and don't create any of your own. If you are usually the person who starts the drama, spend some time alone to stay at peace with yourself and your unborn baby even if it means sitting at home by yourself. That doesn't mean isolating yourself or going into a state of depression. Use the alone time to get to know things about yourself that you didn't notice while spending time with everyone else. Try sitting in your car at work on your lunch break instead of constantly being surrounded by people and noise. These small steps can help you have more energy and a more pleasant pregnancy. They can also make it easier for you to bounce back after the delivery and be ready to meet the needs of your infant child.

A Father's Influence on Your Baby's Health

If you're already pregnant, then you can't, of course, choose your baby's father based on his habits. However, you should still be aware that the father's habits can affect your baby's health just like your habits can. Is the father loud? Will his voice scare the baby? Is he a smoker of any substance? Does he physically mishandle the baby? Is he likely to take the baby to places that are harmful to the baby or which could even lead to injury or death of the baby? If the answer is yes to any of these questions, you must have a conversation with the father. It will be an unpleasant one, and you may have to take drastic measures to prevent him from being left alone with your child, but whatever you have to do to protect your child must be done. Prepare yourself for it. On the other hand, he may be willing to make major changes and turn out to be the best father ever. Make sure you let him know you appreciate whatever efforts he makes. Men want to be appreciated just like women do. He will need encouragement just as you will.

The Importance of Choosing a Name for Your Child

Naming a child is often a controversial topic. Yes, you can name your child anything you want. You can name him Onion Ring or Apple if you choose to. All I ask is that you consider his future and the challenges he may face when he's independent and trying to make a living. Unfortunately, we live in a world where people judge us every day, and that judgment starts with our names, especially if we are not standing in front of that person who's making the judgment. As soon as people read a name in a news article, see it on a job application, or hear it, they start to make assumptions, especially about race, class, and education. Of course, they're often wrong, but that doesn't change the fact that these assumptions are made and can and will affect your child.

Before my children were born, I put a lot of thought into naming them because I understood how society works. I had to decide if I wanted to defend my children's names at every turn and potentially limit the opportunities that they might have, or allow them to move through life with a focus on showing their character and qualifications. I had to decide whether or not I would allow their names to be a distraction to potential employers and other people with power to influence my children's lives.

Of course, I wanted to set them up for success as much as I could, so I gave my children last names as first names. For example, a name such as Cameron could be used for a girl or a boy, and for any ethnicity. This way, an interviewer will not know if my child is a boy or girl, black or white, or working class or upper class before they meet. My children will be called in for their qualifications and not dismissed due to a name the interviewer cannot pronounce or because the interviewer recognizes their race and decides not to give them the opportunity to interview. I have plans for my children to build wealth and become entrepreneurs, but I am also aware that they may have to start by working for someone else before they can branch out on their own. I chose their names with that in mind.

A person's name tells a story or paints a picture whether you believe it will or not. Sometimes it tells people the person's race, and many people tend to attach negative stereotypes to certain names. Another issue that can deter an interviewer is pronunciation of someone's name. If the interviewer cannot pronounce a name, she may simply pass on the applicant. Many people don't even feel comfortable calling an applicant for an interview when they can't pronounce the candidate's name. They fear humiliating the potential candidate or humiliating themselves. To save themselves from such embarrassment, they just won't call the potential candidate at all. The resume goes in the trash. All because of a name.

Keep in mind your child's role as a potential candidate could mean a candidate for a loan to start her own business, to be named head of an organization, to be considered as a CEO, or to enter a competitive academic program. It's not always to start a job. As your child grows older, she will always be applying for something that can make her life better and help her achieve her goals.

Many parents choose to name children after their fathers. There's no problem with doing so if you think the name is a good one. But before you make that choice, I suggest that you consider the father's reputation in your community and on paper. What kind of credit does he have? Does Dad have a criminal record that can mistakenly appear on your child's record? This can become a hassle for your child if the father doesn't handle his business properly, and it can eventually become a serious problem that impedes your child's path to success. When naming your precious child, keep all of these things in mind. Name your child for himself or herself, not for you or for the father. Have this conversation with the father early on if he wants to name his child after himself. If he understands the potential consequences, he can take the opportunity to correct any issues before naming the child or he may understand why you shouldn't name the child after him all together.

Getting Ready to Bring Your Baby Home

Are you ready to bring your baby home? There are a few things you should purchase or take care of first.

The first thing to purchase is a late-model car seat. Without this, you will not be allowed to leave the hospital with the baby, and your baby should never ride in any vehicle unless she is properly secured in the child safety seat. Do some research on quality, reliable infant car seats. Some have had recalls and could possibly still be on the market, so be careful when you're shopping for one. This is a case when you may want to invest in new rather than buying from a secondhand store or taking a hand-me-down from a friend or relative.

I can't stress enough the amount of antibacterial cleaning products you will need. According to Janitorial Cleaning Services, "Antibacterial cleaning products are useful in healthcare settings where patients' immune systems are weak and hand sanitizers are convenient to use when a person doesn't have access to soap and hot water." [8] If soap and water are readily available, by all means use them instead. Antibacterial products are not a standard cleaning agent. Soap and water is always the best cleaning method.

Visiting family and friends who will touch the baby's hands, feet, and face will bring germs into your home. Guess where the baby will put those hands that the family and friends just touched? You guessed it, in her mouth. There is a disease known as hand-foot-and-mouth disease. (Ask me how I know. My younger daughter contracted it at daycare.) Yes, it is curable, but it is horrible to deal with, so make sure you have plenty of Lysol, antibacterial soap, and wipes. The best precaution is making sure family and friends wash their hands with soap and water before touching your

---

8   Janitorial Cleaning Services. (n.d.). Retrieved November 28, 2016, from http://www.commercialofficecleaning.com/using-antibacterial-cleaning-products.html

baby. Nothing beats soap and water, but make sure the soap is hypoallergenic because they will be touching the baby.

Be aware that some parents choose to not vaccinate their children due to their religious beliefs or because they don't trust the government or pharmaceutical companies. Make sure you do the proper research on vaccines and make a sound decision because your baby's life depends on it. Also, be aware of the risks of exposing your infant child to unvaccinated adults and children, and make decisions accordingly. If your plan is to enroll your child in a daycare or school, ask the daycare workers and schoolteachers about the rules for vaccinations.

Of course, you'll need plenty of bottles, diapers, and wipes. Even if you're exclusively feeding breast milk to your child, you may want or need to pump, so you'll still want to have bottles. If you are not breastfeeding, have plenty of formula on hand for the baby. If at all possible, I suggest you at least try breastfeeding. It provides unique health benefits to your child, and it's great for helping your uterus contract to its normal size as soon as possible.

Choosing a crib is just as important as the other items mentioned, so treat it as such. The wrong crib can be a danger zone for SIDS, falls, suffocation, and germs and bugs. Make sure that the crib you choose has not been recalled and that its design is fit for your home.

As the precious baby gets older, your home design will change, especially once she starts to crawl and walk. As the baby grows, you can visit www.NicolePetite.com and see the list of things to have on hand. I want to help in any way I can. You can also ask me questions on the website, and I'll answer as soon as I can.

As your due date gets closer, make sure you have the essentials you'll need to take care of your baby and keep her safe without putting any extra stress on yourself, the father, or whoever else might be helping you take care of her. Ready or not, here she comes!

Nicole's List of Baby-Readiness Basics

- Infant must-haves:
  - Teething ring
  - Hair brush
  - Baby monitor
  - Rash medication
  - Blankets
  - Socks
  - Hand socks
  - Baby bath soap
  - Baby fingernail clippers
  - Diapers
  - Bottles
  - Baby wipes
  - Infant bathtub
  - Baby washcloths (They are softer than adult washcloths.)
  - Baby toys

- ○ Milk (breast or formula)
- ○ Pacifier (optional)
- ✔ Crawling must-haves:
  - ○ Socket covers
  - ○ Disinfectant
  - ○ Knee pads (optional)
  - ○ Baby gates
  - ○ Sippy cups
  - ○ Child-size chairs
- ✔ New walker must-haves:
  - ○ Walking shoes (not Nike or Jordans)
  - ○ Bumpers or cushions on tables and other sharp edges or corners

LESSON 2

No Longer Alone

Your family and friends have now all left your home, and it's just you, your baby, and the baby's father—or just you and the baby. What do you do? Don't panic. Remember you have bonded with this precious life from conception, so a lot of this parenting thing will come naturally for you. You got this. Take a seat, breathe for a few minutes, and get your head back in the game.

Infancy and Toddlerhood

If you don't feel like you've bonded with your baby yet, or if you're having feelings of depression, intense irritability or anger, extreme mood swings, or other unusual emotional symptoms, please see a doctor right away. These can be some of the symptoms of postpartum depression, and you need to see a medical professional for help. Tell a close friend or family member what you're experiencing and how you're seeking help.

If there is a dad in the home or closely involved with the child you share, his bond with the child is just as important as yours. Many men feel it is the mother's place to raise the baby. They mistakenly think they don't need to participate until the baby gets older. That is so far from the truth. When a father connects with his baby, a bond is formed that helps the father parent naturally. His fatherly instincts kick in, and he becomes more aware of what the child needs. It also gives the child another place to turn to have his needs met, and gives you help with the child-raising responsibilities. Allow the father time with the baby. Maybe when you are resting, he's bonding and raising his child as he see fit. He needs to be just as involved as mommy. That kind of arrangement will benefit all three of you.

If there is no father around and it's just you, it's okay (same as if the mother is not present). Don't beat yourself up or blame the dad for not being there. Accept reality, and keep moving. If you build up resentment about the father's absence, you will take it out on that baby. As a mother, once you find out you're pregnant, you have to shift your concern from the father to that child. If you do not, the child will suffer before and after birth. How do you move on? The first thing you must do is realize that you can raise your child to be a noble, successful, and productive person with or without the father's help.

If the father is absent, understand and know that it's a choice not to be involved in the child's life, and it's his loss. That lack of relationship will have a twofold consequence. The child will not only want and miss her father while she's growing up, but her father will usually yearn for that child once she's an adult. You will not have to badmouth the absent parent, and you shouldn't. Your child will see what her absent parent is or isn't doing.

Remember, it was *your* choice to have sex with the father, so he was obviously good enough in your mind to sleep with at least once. Even if he turned out to be much worse than you thought, you had a choice to wait until you got to know if he was ready to be a parent instead of being ready for sex. You're this baby's mother, and he's the father, so let's move on. Don't dwell on your choice or beat yourself up about it. Realize that you had full control, accept it, and don't blame anyone. Not even yourself. Blame brings resentment, which is unhealthy for you and your baby. This newborn, who will love you unconditionally when no one else will, deserves better.

Now that we have that out of the way, you should be able to clear your head for what's to come.

Infancy

During this stage, from one day to twelve months, you and the baby's other caregivers should pay attention to the baby and interact with her by talking to her, smiling with her, hugging her, and having plenty of soft music and soft voice

Leave an "I love you" note in his book bag in the morning.

time with the baby. If you are loud with the child, the child will become uneasy and will likely become loud too. Earlier I shared how my brother is loud and his daughter is loud too. You should be careful of the energy around you and your baby at all times. Of course, you cannot be with your baby twenty-four hours a day, especially if you have to go back to work, but most of the baby's time should be spent with you, not grandma, aunties, or friends—you. This gives you the opportunity to be the biggest influence in your child's life, which is vital.

Infancy is a critical time in that baby's life, as well as yours. What you instill in this child during infancy will affect his or her character and choices later in life. In the early days, you may or may not get much sleep. Both of my babies slept a lot in the beginning. I had to wake them up just to feed them. Sometimes it scared me that they slept so much. On the other hand, your baby may not be a sleeper. This is something you should prepare for during pregnancy. I do believe if you lived a calm life while the baby was inside of you, the baby will probably be calm when he or she is born. This is simply what I've observed in my own experience.

Make sure when holding your baby that you are holding her correctly and give her a chance to feel you and your heartbeat. Spending more time touching and loving on your baby makes him more comfortable, secures the bond, and helps grow trust. The baby begins to notice how you feel as well as how you naturally smell when you walk into a room. Putting your baby in a rocker all the time, in my opinion, can make the baby insensible and insecure. I know the old saying is "Don't hold him all the time. You'll spoil him." But don't misinterpret that saying by never holding the baby or having other skin-touching moments. They are babies. They need that.

As the child gets older, you should observe his habits to determine which habits should be broken, such as sucking his thumb, biting others, putting everything in his mouth, repeating curse words he has heard, kissing everyone he meets, and other habits that can be problematic. You should also be aware of how your child interacts with others. Pay attention to your child's growth and developmental skills. Things he should be doing throughout the first year include:

- Teething
- Smiling/laughing
- Tracking faces with eyes
- Sitting up
- Crawling
- Scooting
- Picking up items
- Trying to walk or already walking
- Trying to speak. Words such as mama and dada should be clear.
- Visual – Making sure that they are seeing the right colors, making sure they are seeing properly up close and not straining to see objects in front of them.
- Displaying a range of emotions

🡢 Developing good eating habits, which includes a diet high in fruits and vegetables once solid foods are added.

These are just a few things to pay close attention to while your baby is growing. During this time, your child's doctor should keep you informed of appropriate developmental milestones but it's still crucial that you spend more time with your child than anyone else does. You can't observe your child's development if you're not spending time with him. If there is an active father around, he too needs to form a bond with the child and pay attention to the child's development. Whether it's a boy or a girl, the father's role is just as important as the mother's. Just like you, the father needs to take responsibility for the influences in the child's surroundings and pay attention to the growth of the child. A happy baby is developed through the connections he forms and the quality of his surroundings. Make them positive. Your child's life depends on it.

Dangers. There are potential dangers associated with having an infant. It's important to be aware of them so you can take the necessary steps to protect your child to the best of your ability. One such danger is sudden infant death syndrome or SIDs. According to Mayo Clinic, the items in a baby's crib and his or her sleeping position can combine with known or unknown physical problems to increase the risk of SIDS. Risk factors include the following:

- Sleeping on the stomach or side. Babies who are placed on their stomachs or sides to sleep may have more difficulty breathing than those placed on their backs.
- Sleeping on a soft surface. Lying face down on a fluffy comforter or a waterbed can block an infant's airway. Draping a blanket over a baby's head is especially risky.
- Sleeping with parents. While the risk of SIDS is lowered if an infant sleeps in the same room as his or her parents, the risk increases if the baby sleeps in the same bed. This is partly due to the fact there are more soft surfaces in an adult bed that can impair breathing.
- Cigarette and other smoke. The toxins in smoke make it difficult for babies to get enough oxygen and can damage their hearts and brains.

While the exact cause of SIDS in any given case may be difficult to pinpoint, any of these factors can put a baby at greater risk of sudden infant death syndrome.[9] You have it within your control to reduce the risks to your child. Do everything you can to improve her odds of making it to her toddler years and beyond.

From the very beginning, you need to be aware of the words you choose to use with and in front of your small child. What you call him is what he will become, so you must avoid the use of profanity out of respect to your child and never

---

9 Sudden infant death syndrome (SIDS) Causes. (n.d.). Retrieved March 02, 2017, from http://www.mayoclinic.org/diseases-conditions/sudden-infant-death-syndrome/basics/causes/CON-20020269

verbally (or physically) abuse your child. Never. If there is ever a time where you cannot take it anymore, please call a close family member, friend, or child services and allow them to remove your children. If you just need time alone, find a responsible adult you trust to leave your child with, and take a few days to decompress and renew your energy. Remember, no one is perfect, and we all need time away to be at our best. Don't feel as if that's bad parenting. The ability to recognize your breaking point before you actually break something or someone is actually a great parenting skill!

Toddlerhood (ages 2 to 5)

Now you have a child running around the house, pulling things off the table, climbing on the furniture, running and falling, spilling food everywhere, putting herself in danger, everywhere she turns, without a care in the world. Don't panic. These are the times when her little brain is moving so fast her little legs can't keep up. This is the perfect time to engage her in learning colors, numbers, letters, listening to stories, and singing songs. Contrary to popular belief, a toddler can consume and learn great amounts of information before turning three years old, so use that time wisely!

The sooner you start to teach your child, the more prepared and advanced she will be when the time comes for her to begin her formal education. What is most important about this stage in your child's life is what you introduce her to on a regular basis. For example, picture books and music are very important to a child at this age. Toys designed to help your child develop can be beneficial, especially when you use them as a fun way to engage with your child. This is a great time to help your child develop a love of books by reading picture books and other age-appropriate books together.

TV, Video Games, and Electronics

I am not a big fan of keeping your baby entertained with television and other electronic devices. One reason is that it has been proven to be bad for your child's eyes. They tend to go from the TV to the videogames, back to the TV, and then to the cell phones. This can hinder the normal development of their eyesight. Another reason why I would not recommend allowing these items to entertain your child is because, at this point, the electronic babysitter begins to raise your child. It is called programming for a reason. At this age, your child will absorb so much and before she's mature enough to know how to separate fiction and nonfiction. Limit screen time, and give your child games that allow her to use her brain and have fun at the same time.

Sibling Love

Do you have more than one child? Do they have different fathers or mothers? How do we teach siblings to be close and love each other unconditionally and take care of each other? Some parents, unconsciously, make the siblings compete with each other for the parents' attention or show more love to one than the other. This immediately builds wedges between them and resentment and anger starts to form.

Demonstrating favoritism by giving more attention or more love to one child as compared to the other will almost always push the siblings apart.

Bonding between your children can show them love and attention from each other and uplift them equally. You also need to punish them equally. If you single out one child for more punishment, that child will feel ostracized and angry. If that child is actually doing things that get her in trouble more often, you should encourage your other child (or children) to work with you to help that child get things in order. That way, everyone will participate in giving that child more of the attention she's probably seeking. It will be a family effort. The important thing is that your children understand that they are all equally loved by you, family comes first, and their sibling bond is unbreakable.

Building Self-Esteem

Every child needs parents who fuel her self-esteem. If you're raising a child from any minority group, then it's especially important to boost the self-esteem of this child from the beginning of her life. She will be introduced to enough negative imagery, impossible standards of beauty, and cultural prejudices that say she isn't good enough from the media and society at large. She needs early positive reinforcement from you. (While I'm using the feminine pronoun here, let me reiterate that all of this applies to boys and girls equally.) Tell her all the time how beautiful she is. Tell her she's smart and that she can do anything. Your child needs your help to build a solid foundation of healthy self-esteem. Make sure you provide positive feedback and affirmation so she knows her worth from the earliest age. All children need this.

Your child is learning to trust you and will come to you with any little problem she may have such as a "boo boo" from a fall or scrape, a request for a snack, or if she simply needs a hug. When you respond appropriately, you build her confidence that she can trust that you or her daddy will fix any problem she has. Never shun or belittle your child when she comes to you for help. Her ability to rely on you helps the two of you grow closer, and the child begins to understand what love truly is.

Raising a Black Child

As always, it's critical to make sure you are not using profanity with or around the child and you are not demeaning the child in any fashion. Make sure that no one else is referring to your child with any derogatory or demeaning terms. I've added this section as I once was a black child and I am very aware of the obstacles faced on a regular basis so I felt as if I should speak on it. It's only fair. If you are raising a black child, please be sure no one is referring to your child as a "nigga" or any other derogatory name, and teach him that those words are not terms of endearment. Teach him about his history by talking about it and reading relevant books together. Teach him the history that will never be taught in the conventional history books, including stories like the massacre at "Black Wall Street," in Tulsa, Oklahoma, the lynching of Emmett Till, and the Tuskegee Experiment. Teach him about the Middle Passage. Also, teach him about events like Juneteenth and the accomplishments of his people in the face of systemic oppression. There are so many significant historical events that will never be taught in school that he can learn. Having that knowledge can boost your child's self-esteem. Any child of a different ethnicity should be taught about where she comes from and how her people have contributed to society. It is important for her to know her roots. Pride is often born from knowing who you are.

The only black history most children learn in school is a watered-down history of slavery, which is a limited perspective that can actually damage their sense of self-worth, so make sure you teach cultural pride and not negativity. The world will provide enough of the negativity for you. Do not add to it. Uplift this child with your words and the music and images that surround her. Tell her how strong she is and that she can be anything she wants to be in this world.

Discipline, Personality, and Character in Your Toddler

At this stage, you are also helping your child understand what behavior is acceptable and what is not. You want to reward her for doing something good, but you also want to discipline her for doing something you do not want her to do again. Appropriately disciplining a toddler can go a long way. You should never discipline out of anger but only to ensure a lesson is learned. Any discipline should be accompanied by a conversation because your child needs to know and understand why she's being disciplined.

When my older daughter was ten months old, I found her getting into the bathroom cabinet, where all the dangerous cleaning products were. She used to crawl into the bathroom and try to take out the bottles and cans. I watched her and grabbed her each time, so she never harmed herself. I could have easily moved the products, but I chose to make this a lesson instead. One day, when she went back to the cabinet, I tapped her hand. She didn't cry, but it shocked her. She looked up at me as if to say, "Mama! What did you just do to me?" I repeated the word no, and she crawled away. I never had to make her leave the cabinet again. Luckily for me it worked. The purpose of not moving the dangerous products was because wherever I moved them, she might, somehow, find them again. She would not have had learned to not bother them.

That kind of discipline worked for me because I had been observing my daughter enough to know what would work and what would not. Some children are stubborn and a little bit more carefree, and a tap on the hand may not work for them, but if you are observing your child from birth, you already know whether or not a tap will not work for her. What worked for my older child did not work for my younger daughter. She has always been the stubborn one. She is one who will keep touching the fire until she is burned to a crisp and then ask how it happened. Every child is different and learns in different ways, so observe your child and discipline her according to her specific personality.

You can easily open up a line of communication with your toddler. Children are already very inquisitive at that age. Let the questions rip! Never tell your child to "hush" or "stop asking questions." When a child starts to ask questions, you have his undivided attention and an opportunity to teach lessons that he will never forget. If, for whatever reason, you cannot answer the question and engage in a conversation with your child in the moment, *always* come back to it. That builds character in your child, it builds self-esteem in your child, and it allows your child to feel as if he matters from the earliest possible age.

During the toddler years, your child is already developing his character and personality traits. However, you should also be aware that he experiences the full range of human emotions and can become angry, sad, or depressed. If your child is attending daycare, the daycare providers should pick up any significant emotional changes immediately. A good day care provider will talk to you about any worrisome behaviors or moods your child displays, and you should be open to listening. At the same time, you should watch for any such changes in your child because they could indicate that he's having trouble adjusting or is being mistreated in day care. A child can even show if he's being beaten or abused by someone based on the way he withdraws or acts up when that person is around.

Raising a Positive (or Negative) Adult from the Beginning

Since you will be his primary influence, ask yourself what your child thinks of you. If he could write a summary about who you are as a parent, what would he say? What would the child complain about that he thinks you do wrong? I say "think" because you may actually being doing it right. Your child simply doesn't understand it yet. There were quite a few things I thought my mom did wrong as I growing up, but I got the *aha moments* and understood her reasoning when I became an adult and a mom. What does your child love most about you? Would he say he feels safe with you and can rely on you? Or does he sometimes wonder if you'll take your problems out on him?

Your child will not be in your presence all the time, so you have to trust and believe that what you instill in him, he will take wherever he goes. I can confidently say that when my children are not with me, or with any other adult, that I would generally be proud of any decisions they make. I say *generally* because there is always at least one person or situation that can make your child go against his will or his morals. Always.

A toddler with a bad attitude is usually depicting the attitude of those who are raising him, or he may be dealing with underlying, much more concerning issues. Either way, it needs to be dealt with, and it must start with you, the parent. As an adult, if you find your toddler's behavior leaning towards something that you do not approve of, what should you do? I would clear my schedule of any extracurricular activities that I have for myself for a while and focus on giving my child my undivided attention. If you are not used to spending time with your child or listening to your child, in one day you will learn so much about him by doing exactly that. The most important thing you can do for your child is to listen. The next important thing you can do is lead. No, I don't necessarily mean lead by example, but you do have to lead.

Some habits are hard to break as an adult, so it is hypocritical to tell a child not to smoke when you go through a pack of cigarettes a day. Children will always *hear* what you say but *listen* to what you do. For example, telling a child not to smoke while blowing your cigarette smoke out the window is just dumb. The way you would handle that, with a child of any age, is to tell your child not to smoke, while explaining the addiction you have. Tell him you would love to be able to stop soon because you know it's bad for your health. Make sure you stick to your word and make a real effort to break your addiction.

That's how you lead, while not leading by example. Leading by example is way overrated because humans, even parents, are flawed. That kind of leadership should not be given so much emphasis. Once you begin to understand that we are human first, you can accept that it is okay for our children to see us make mistakes. It's not the mistakes we make, it's how we overcome them that will most significantly influence our children.

Respect for Others and Self-Respect

So often I hear people say, "You have to earn respect in order to receive it." I am still trying to find the person who started this rumor because it doesn't make any sense to me. Respect should be given whenever you meet someone. They don't have to earn it. Now, you may lose respect for someone based on their actions and attitude, but it definitely doesn't need to be earned. Teach your child from an early age to respect others. Teach him basic manners, like saying please and thank you, and insist that he use them from an early age. At the same time, teach him that he is deserving of the same treatment from the people who interact with him. He should grow up expecting to be treated with the same respect he gives others. Once a child shows a standard of respect that he gives himself, people around him will generally give that respect upon meeting him.

Outside Influences

At this age, children are true sponges. They pick up and quickly learn and absorb whatever they see, hear, and experience around them, so be very careful. I didn't curse around my children when they were this age, but I do now that they are much older. At this point, they are mature enough to understand my stress load, and sometimes a little profanity actually breaks the tension and makes them feel relieved. However, I don't curse *at* them, just as a part of a conversation, maybe on the phone with a friend or a family member. I was careful not to curse around them when they were too young to understand the distinction between me cursing at them and me cursing about something going on in my life. That meant I also had to keep them away from people, music, and media that would introduce them to that language.

Children will idolize whoever they feel is around to protect them, love them, and make them happy. A lot of parents are content to allow their children to idolize Santa Claus, superheroes, and other fantasy images. At one point, I realized that my first child's idol was a fictional man created by society named Santa Claus. Idolizing him took away from her appreciation of the people who were truly responsible for making her so happy during that particular holiday. I had to ask myself why I would allow my child to think some man who was coming down our chimney (which we didn't have) and delivering toys to her (that we paid for), was responsible for putting that Christmas-morning smile on her face. We were cheating ourselves of that moment of joy and appreciation and giving it to an imaginary image. That stopped as soon as I realized it was happening.

Of course, not all parents feel this way, and many are perfectly okay with the Santa Claus fantasy. That's your choice to make. Nothing wrong with a child being a child. Santa Claus is part of an old tradition that many families carry on. Please be aware that some children are cruel and will tell your child Santa Claus is not real. When your child asks you, you'll have to decide if you will tell your child the truth or if you will continue to keep up the tradition in the face of the evidence that Santa isn't real. That's totally up to you. Some children know Santa is not real and will play along to make you happy.

At first, my girls were in awe when they found out that Santa did not exist and we were the culprits behind the gifts, but they quickly embraced us and thanked us for what we had done for them. That gratitude gave us joy and a sense that they both appreciated what we had done for them. I watched their admiration grow for us as their parents. After that, during holidays, they bought us gifts to show us how thankful they were of us. Children should learn, at an early age, who will be their provider and who they can depend on. This builds trust, love, and admiration. When you give credit to outside sources for the things you do, you diminish the sense of dependency and appreciation your children should have for you.

Why You Must...

There are some things that you must do in the very beginning so you don't run the risk of losing total control over the raising of your own child.

Put the proper fear in your child at an early age. If you do not do this early on, he will not respect you. When a child is so young, the communication between the two of you is limited, and trying to converse with a toddler to convince him to behave or to do something you want him to do can get complicated. I put fear in my children when they were as young as ten months old. Earlier, I shared how I tapped my daughter's hand for going under the bathroom sink and trying to play with (and potentially drink) toxic cleaning fluids. I wanted her to be afraid to do it again. At such a young age, toddlers understand fear, not reasoning. And that's okay, as long as it is not abusive.

Demonstrate love after disciplining your child. If you are always punishing your child without reminding him that you love him, the child starts to build resentment and disrespect for you, and he will soon start trying to get what he wants with manipulation. Even today, when I punish my teenager, I make sure that the lines of communication are open. I ensure that she understands why she is being punished and that she knows it has nothing to do with me being angry. I am usually upset when I punish her, but I always come back during the punishment and have a civil conversation with her about the actions that got her on punishment in the first place. I always leave her with a reminder that I discipline her because I love her.

I am not afraid to say that I get angry with my children. You know why? Because I have accepted that I am human, and my children know that too. I don't punish out of anger, and punishment is not always the answer to a child's inappropriate actions. Typically, a combination of communication and punishment works the best. Because we talk and she knows I love and care about her, my daughter is now more concerned about disappointing me with bad choices or behavior than she is about getting punished. I tend to express my disappointment and let her know when her behavior has let me down. That gives her the motivation to do better since I am one of the people she wants to impress.

Allow your child to see you happy. The person or people your child is around the most will determine the emotions he's exposed to the most. An unhappy parent will create an unhappy child. A happy parent will create a happy child if that child spends most of his time with that parent. So if you are spending most of your free time with your child, as you should be, being happy will allow him to go into the world being happy about life instead of walking around with a chip on his shoulder without even understanding why it's there.

Listen to your child without preparing to respond. He knows more than you think he knows, and you should always give him a chance to talk to you about how he feels and why he feels that way. The best thing you can do for your child is to listen to him, even when he's very young. Do not be the parent who's busy forming a rebuttal before your child finishes expressing his thoughts to you. Then you become "that parent who doesn't listen." And guess what happens? As your child grows older, he will find another outlet to express his thoughts and start to lose interest in any advice you can give him. That is the worst thing that can happen because you will no longer be his biggest influence. I am not saying you have to agree with your child, but you must allow him to get out what he wants to say without interruption and sarcasm. Make sure you let him get his thoughts and feelings out without cutting him off or being condescending.

Molding Your Child's Daily Habits

Most of your child's days are made up of repeated actions and activities. These create habits that your child takes on naturally. I taught my daughters to say "yes ma'am" and "no ma'am," "yes sir" and "no sir," to say grace and nightly prayers, and to eat as many healthy foods as possible. One thing I didn't do, and really wish I had, was get them used to drinking water. That turned out to be a hard task because I didn't introduce them to it at an early age. This leads me to four things that you should monitor throughout your child's life, starting from the toddler years.

- Make sure your child is exposed to and eats a variety of healthy foods. As she grows older, your child will be more likely to want to eat the foods you introduced to her at an early age. Of course, sometimes that will change. As the parent, you have to make sure your child is getting the proper nutrition from the best possible food sources. Obesity has become an epidemic, and it is usually strictly due to what we allow our children to eat. When you give your child fruits and vegetables from a young age, you're essentially setting her palette and creating a desire for those foods for the rest of her life. The same applies when you give your child chicken nuggets, french fries, chips, candy, and soda on a regular basis. You're helping her to develop a lifelong love of those foods, which can lead to a lifelong struggle with weight and weight-related issues. You can teach your child to enjoy drinking water or you can train her to crave soda. It's up to you. You are the parent. Sometimes those habits can backfire, and when your children get to a certain age they will hate what they were taught to eat growing up. If for nothing else, they will know what foods are healthy and hopefully go back to them as they mature.

- When it comes to your child's health, food and exercise go hand in hand. We all know that these days, many children do not enjoy going outside to play as we did growing up. A lot of children may never know how to ride a bike, swim, or jump rope. They spend so much time playing video games or just lying around the house watching videos or wasting time on social media. For the first several years, your child will need you to go outside and play with her, take her to a park or playground, and teach her basic games. Playing outdoors with her will help her learn to love physical activity. There are several reasons for you to participate. One reason is to bond. Another is to protect her.

- As your child gets older, she can engage in extracurricular activities to get more physical activity. Dance, martial arts, and team sports are a few good choices. These activities have the added benefits of keeping her out of trouble while helping her discover who she is and what she enjoys. Your child may decide to choose a sport that is not your favorite, but it may teach her important lifelong skills or even win her a full scholarship at a university. Don't discourage her from choosing an unpopular sport. She's much more likely to stick with something she enjoys than the sport you force her to play.

➢ Last, remember that reading is essential for your child's health, just like food and exercise. This is a subject that I emphasize because a lot of children, many of the underprivileged boys and girls, are not reading on the level they should be reading on.[10] You can usually tell this by the way they speak. As a parent, it is your responsibility to make sure your child is on track to go to the next grade level prepared to do the work, and that includes reading at or above that grade level. Without the proper reading skills, she will not succeed. In the toddler years, you should read your child the books she enjoys and take her to visit libraries or bookstores. Encourage her to fill in some of the words of her favorite books as you read to her. If you start at a young age, she will be much more likely to develop a love of reading. As she gets older, of course, her reading

---

10 Gabriel, T. (2010, November 08). Proficiency of Black Students Is Found to Be Far Lower Than Expected. Retrieved March 02, 2017, from http://www.nytimes.com/2010/11/09/education/09gap.html

choices will change. Make sure your child has access to books. This is your responsibility.

The toddler years can be challenging, but many parents have made it through them successfully, and so can you. It takes time, effort, and awareness of your child's needs, but when you're willing to put in the work, you'll lay a strong foundation on which your child can stand for the rest of her life. Enjoy this time with your young child. Before you know it, she will be moving on to the preschool years.

LESSON 3
Preschool Years (Ages 3 to 5)

You have survived the period of time of being with your baby with little interference from the outside world. You have successfully accomplished getting your baby to the preschool stage. Hopefully you have taught your child many of the essentials preschoolers need to know. He should know simple things such as his age, how to count to ten, and some basic shapes and colors. Visit my blog, at www.NicolePetite.com.com, and download a list of things a toddler should know and do so you can stay on track with your child's development.

Early Learning

At this age, children should be reading some simple words. These words should be words that are used daily such as "and," "are," "or," and "the." The United States seems to be so far behind other countries when it comes to encouraging our children to develop their intellectual gifts. Our educational achievements lag behind those of many development nations. If you think of the scientists, doctors, and professors in America, a great many of them are foreign and have come here to work or continue their education. They are able to do that because of the educational foundation they were given early in life. Don't hesitate to attempt to teach your child skills and information that American children typically wait to learn. Give your child the opportunity, and he'll let you know if he's ready or not.

Your child may or may not have attended day care. Some parents are skeptical about putting their child in day care these days. That's very understandable, so I won't try to convince you to put your precious baby into one. If, by some chance, you do know and trust a day care, then full-time or part-time attendance can be a great way for your child to learn to adapt to new environments and interact with other children, especially if you're raising an only child. If you can help it, you do not want your child to get to kindergarten and be forced to begin his formal education while having to learn to adapt to being around other children at the same time. Adapting to a new environment and trying to learn can be traumatizing for the child, or it can be easy. It depends on your child's personality. During these years, you have to at least let go of a pinky, even if you still have the other nine fingers in your hand.

If you are spending time with your child, you are probably aware of how fast or how slowly your preschooler learns. This is a crucial period in her life because it helps to determine what type of learner your child will be as she grows up. The sooner you can determine that, the more you can teach your child, and the faster and more she can learn. Interaction and observation also allow you to determine if your child may be dealing with any disabilities and how they can be overcome. The earlier you can detect a disability (stuttering is one example), the higher the chances of your child learning to adapt to it.

Who and What Is Influencing Your Child?

If you haven't already, you need to become careful about what your child consumes on the radio, television, and the Internet. Much of the current rap music being aired on local airwaves is horrible, and many of the rappers are no longer even saying words found in the English language. The words you do understand are usually not pleasant words to repeat. There is some very positive rap music available, but this music is usually not on the radio. If it is, it's not played very often or often enough. Some positive rap artists who come to mind are lyricists like Common, Nas, J. Cole, and Lecrae, just to name a few. Other genres of music lyrics can be harsh as well for your baby to repeat. Make sure you aren't careless with what your child listens to because she will pick it up fast and most definitely repeat it. Commit to wisely choosing the music you will expose your child to. Listen with your baby. Of course, you won't be able to monitor everything your child listens to or sees when he's with other family members or exposed to the Internet. That brings me to the next point as to how you can be comfortable when he does hear negative music or see or hear things you'd rather he didn't.

Monitoring television is just as important. There is so much sexual content and violence on television today that it can be harsh for such young minds. Remember, television is called "programming" for a reason. Monitor your child's television shows and educate them about why you choose to avoid them because they will see these shows somewhere. If they know up front that it is all fake, they may be able to discern between real life and acting.

We also have to pay attention to the internet. You can find anything on the internet these days, and if children have access to smart phones, they have access to everything. Social media falls into this category as well.

I made sure my children understood that the rappers and other celebrities they saw and heard were only actors and didn't live the lifestyles they presented on TV. As long as my girls understood this, I wasn't really worried about them mimicking habits of the rappers and other music artists. Those habits can affect your child's development, including how he speaks or walks and what he's willing to try because the actors make it look fun. You have to remember you are dealing with immature minds. Do your best to be aware of what your child listens to when he's not with you, and address it even at this early age. Whatever your child is learning outside the home he will surely bring it back to you, so pay attention.

When my children were this age, I would always ask them what all they did that day if they were away with either of their grannies or any other family member. Typically, once you ask a child that question, especially at a young age, they are like a water faucet. They will tell you everything! It's a beautiful thing because they will even tell about things that didn't even pertain to them or affect them in any way. Try it. You will be amazed at what they share with you.

Once, I asked my oldest child that question, and she told me that Granny ate some food and then took it out of her mouth and gave it to my younger daughter. I died and came back to life. I'm almost sure that whenever I become a grandmother, I will probably do the same (not really). At the time, that grossed me out, and I tried to figure out a way to stop my child from receiving food from her grandmother that way. Granny was simply trying to make sure the food wasn't too hot before my daughter put it in her mouth, but I was still a little freaked out about it. If I hadn't asked my daughter what happened that day, I would have never known about it. So ask away. Of course, your child may tell you some things that you didn't want to know, so be prepared.

How you react to your child and how you respond verbally to her also plays a major role in how her character forms and whether or not she develops any unhealthy defense mechanisms. In today's society, many children appear to be very angry. One can only assume this attitude often stems from the negative behavior of someone they are very close to, whether it's a parent cursing or yelling at them all the time or from other circumstances the children cannot correct themselves, such as not having water, lights, or other basic necessities. If there is any domestic abuse going on in the home, it will definitely shape the child's character and influence who he or she will become, and it can create anger issues a young child has no idea how to deal with. Those characteristics can change as the child grows and matures, but having to deal with an angry child can lead to bad decisions during this stage.

Your Child's Natural Interest in Learning

Every day is a day to teach a preschooler something new. Never be afraid to teach your child something that you feel he should learn in greater depth later in life or something you feel he may not be fully capable of understanding yet. You may just be surprised by what he'll learn and what he'll gravitate to once he learns it. Some examples of these teachable moments would be something like learning the name of a certain insect they see, or how leather was created, or how money is made. These are everyday items that can spark a child's curiosity, and you will be surprised by how far they will take it once they are intrigued. No subject is too complex once it has their attention.

It is always best, in my opinion, to teach your child as much as he is able to absorb because it opens up ways for him to start imagining, even as young as three years old, what he may want to do with his life after high school. It's never too early to start this process. At this age, children are usually inquisitive, and they ask so many questions. The worst thing you can do is ignore their questions.

Luckily for my children and me, I am just as inquisitive (or you could say just as nosey) as my children were at this age. I was happy to stop and entertain their questions, and I made sure that they were able to interact with me by asking more questions as I responded, creating an ongoing conversation. I also did my best to make sure they understood my answers as much as possible. One day, I was in Sears with my three-year-old daughter. She asked me, "Mommy, what is gravity?" I had just dropped a shoe I was trying on, and she asked what made the shoe fall. My answer was gravity, so her question followed. I commenced to explain to her exactly what gravity is. An older woman overheard our discussion and came up to tell me I shouldn't be explaining such a complicated concept to my daughter at such a young age.

I'll censor what I said to this stranger because I wouldn't recommend you doing the same and blaming me for your response. Let's just say I rejected the woman's advice. There is no wrong age to explain to your child what he wants to learn. In fact, the best time to explain something to him is when he's asking about it. In those moments, you have his undivided attention, and you may learn something about your child in that conversation that you would have never otherwise known. So please, by all means, slow down and converse with your nosey child.

The difficult part of this kind of engagement with your child is figuring out how to answer questions when a child asks you about things that could possibly do them harm. Before answering these types of questions, you need to have a feel for what type of character your child has, and most importantly, who your child wants to please. Does your child do things to make you happy just to see you smile? Is there someone else your child wants to please? Keep those things in mind when you answer questions about potentially harmful subjects.

Even at this young age, your child may ask you about seeing someone do drugs in real life or on television or the Internet. If you do anything but tell you child the truth, you are doing an injustice to your child and to yourself. Once you give him the honest answer, explain to your child what the answer means to you. Hopefully, what you say and how you feel means a lot to your child. If it doesn't, you will need to get the person who does matter to agree with whatever you say. The messenger matters a lot to a child, and important messages need to come from someone he respects.

Hug and kiss her good-night and whenever she leaves the house.

If your child is asking you questions and you don't answer them honestly or answer them at all, he will get the answer from the streets, especially as he gets older—and the streets are harsh. Pay attention to what your preschool-aged child asks about and what he may be learning from someone or somewhere else. Just as he asks you questions, ask him questions to find out what he knows about tough subjects. As long as you are engaging in conversation with him and teaching the truth along the way, the two of you should be just fine.

Child-Led Interests

Once children start to ask questions, they begin to discover what they may have an interest in. As your child does this, feed that interest, whether you are interested in the same things or not. An idle mind is dangerous for a child to have, so if your son expresses an interest in something that will only lead to more knowledge, allow him the room to explore. Buy age-appropriate books for the subjects your child is most interested in; you can even buy advanced books. If he's hungry for the information, you will be surprised by what he'll teach himself. At this age, your child may express an interest in things that you, as an adult, never thought about. In that case, you can learn along with him.

Dealing with Discrimination

Your child will face discrimination early in life, starting in preschool, whether she's black, white, green, purple, or orange. Whether your family belongs to the upper class or the middle class, someone out there will have a problem with your child based on that background. Teach your child how to deal with people who treat her unfairly, and she will eventually learn to stand for what's right when she sees injustice being done to others.

How will your black or Hispanic child deal with the race-based tension with police? How will your child deal with racial or religious discrimination if she's black, Muslim, or Native American? How will your child handle gender discrimination (which can happen to both boys and girls)?

How does your daughter or son react to domestic violence? Talk about it. Has your child been exposed to it or been a victim of it? These are conversations that must be had from an early age, and as parents, teachers, uncles, aunts, and mentors, we must sit with the children in our lives and tell them the truth about our society so they can handle these challenges in a safe, positive way.

Early Work Ethic

A preschooler should be picking up his toys and taking his plate to the sink after a meal on his own most of the time. An exception would be when he's ill. Teaching a child responsibility from the earliest age teaches character and good habits. This gives the child a sense of independence, and his increasing level of responsibility should be rewarded accordingly. When they were young, my children didn't understand why I made them clean up, and when they got older, they asked me to explain my reasons to them, which I did.

I explained to my daughters that once it becomes second nature for a person to do something, she will typically carry that habit with her throughout life. I never gave them chores as a punishment. I know a few parents who do, and it's an easy way to make children not want to ever clean up when they're grown and gone. I needed to be certain that my children would know how to clean up after themselves and understand why that habit was an important one. I also thought about my daughters' future college days. Knowing that they would likely have roommates, I didn't want my children to be the nasty students in the dorm room. (Some of you have experienced nasty roommates, so you understand.) More importantly, my girls need to be able to clean up after themselves when they eventually get their own places, and eventually keep a clean home for their own families while teaching their children to do the same.

The chart below lists age-appropriate chores for preschoolers. Choose a few to let your child help you with. Don't expect him to do a perfect job at this age. The point is to help him develop a sense of responsibility and pride in his work.

Bedroom chores	✔ Put toys back in their proper place. ✔ Put clothes in drawers after they are folded. ✔ Vacuum. ✔ Attempt to make bed.
Living room chores	✔ Dust tables and chairs. ✔ Vacuum. ✔ Fluff sofa pillows. ✔ Clear room of any items that do not belong in the living area. ✔ Water plants.
Kitchen chores	✔ Put dishes in dishwasher. ✔ Wipe counters off with disinfectant wipes. ✔ Put all trash in the trashcan. ✔ Sweep.
Bathroom chores	✔ Wipe off counters with disinfectant. ✔ Wipe out the tub after they have used it. ✔ Sweep.
Yard chores	✔ Sweep porch and sidewalk. ✔ Rake leaves. ✔ Help an adult with gardening tasks.

Warning: Changes in Behavior

As a preschooler, your child is now mingling with other children, especially if she's in day care or if she's spending time with other family members who have children. Now you must focus on how your child interacts with others and assess whether she has the characteristics to be a leader or a follower. This will give you a good idea of how easily she may be influenced by other children now and in the future. Does she easily pick up language you don't allow in your home? Does she take on bad habits, like hitting, spitting, or biting? Is she the one who, positively or negatively, influences other children? You are building a foundation for your child's character, so ask questions and pay attention.

If your child is in day care, observe her when she doesn't know you're watching to see how she interacts with other children when you're not around. What you see may surprise you. Always be objective and never become that parent who says, "My child will never _____." That is one of the biggest mistakes a parent can make. It's a way to deny or avoid issues that your child may be having. The best way to avoid that pitfall is to watch your child when she's unaware of your presence. If you start checking in on her school behavior early in her life, she will understand that you could be watching at any time. She will also recognize, and eventually appreciate, that you care about her education and well-being enough to always be around and be aware.

Make sure you take time to understand your child's unique personality and how she interacts with children and

adults. For example, some children can be too friendly. Their parents need to teach them how to avoid dangerous or inappropriate contact with strangers. Once you've gotten a grasp on your child's personality and people skills, you must correct any behaviors that are harmful to your child or others. For instance, has your child become a bully? Has your daughter picked up bad habits, such as lying or stealing from another child? Is she developing troublesome characteristics, such as a smart mouth and talking back? These are character flaws that you must—I repeat, *you must*—correct immediately. There is nothing cute about a child using profanity, talking back, or doing anything that challenges your authority as the parent. If you continue to allow those things to happen, you eventually become the child and the child becomes the parent. If you approach the preschool years with an open mind about what your child is capable of and with caution about what she is exposed to, this can be a fun phase for both of you. The foundation you lay during these years can make a huge difference in how successful your child will be in school and in life. However, your job as a parent has only just begun. If your child has already passed preschool age and, looking back, you see a lot you could have done differently, don't beat yourself up. There's plenty you can do to positively influence your child's growth and development as she enters her school years.

LESSON 4

Grammar School (Ages 6 to 10)

You have reached a milestone. This time in your child's life is crucial to his future because he will be exposed to much more than just what you expose him to at home. Your teachings at this point are very important, and you should be confident that what you have taught him thus far will go with him when he is not with you and is faced with peer pressure.

Prepping for the Future by Finding Natural Interests

By this stage of his development, you know a lot about your child's character and personality. You know if he's an extrovert or an introvert. You know if he's outspoken, opinionated, a jokester, a thinker, or a combination of all of these. Once you have determined your child's character and personality, it becomes easier to figure out what he enjoys doing. If your child is an introvert, hopefully you have established trust and have a closeness with him so he will open up to you about his likes and dislikes. It's important that the two of you are able to discuss his preferences openly and honestly.

Sometimes you may have to directly ask if he likes certain things or not. You may just get a shrug of the shoulders. That's okay too. Eventually your child will start asking you for certain things, and those requests all form a pattern of interest. Whatever it is he may gravitate to, this is a great time to start to educate your child about that subject with books, relevant toys or crafts, and exposure to local events. Make sure you monitor his interests because some interests can lead to self-destructive behaviors when they're channeled in the wrong direction or taken too far.

It is never too early to nurture an interest your child has. The more your child gets the chance to experience a niche, the better the chance that it can become a passion that helps him define a future career path. There is nothing more refreshing than making money and building wealth by doing what you love.

Schools and Teachers

When my children were of age to attend school, I specifically looked for small classroom sizes and teachers who were welcoming and engaging, not hostile or cold. Finding the right learning environment for your child at this age (and at every age) is crucial because your child will be formally taught, for the first time, how to read and write. Falling behind in the beginning could leave your child behind for a lifetime. The smaller the class size and better the teacher, the less likely it is that your child will miss out on this foundational instruction.

I also made sure the school was in a decent and safe neighborhood. Children are often outside for recess, and you want to know if there are any predators living nearby or regular violence happening in that neighborhood. The same would be true for a predator on the playground. You would never want your child to encounter a stray bullet while playing innocently outside, doing what children do. Do your research.

Before you choose a school for your son or daughter, take a day to sit in the classroom to make sure the teacher doesn't show any biases. Teachers are human, and they can have biases based on race, gender, religion, class, and other factors, so you want to always make sure your child is being treated fairly, every day. If you're active and involved in your child's education, it will be almost impossible for any teacher to mistreat your child. Your child's teacher should be happy to see that you're a present and involved parent, unless she has another agenda.

Your child will have her own reactions to her new school environment. Just because you feel it's a right fit doesn't mean it is. Of course, as parents we like to believe we always make the best decisions for our children. However, we also have to be considerate of how our children feel in the environment we put them in. If your child isn't comfortable, it will be hard for her to accomplish anything in the classroom. This is another opportunity for you, as a parent, to listen to and learn from your child.

Encourage your child to talk to you about her day at school, and if she has concerns, take them seriously. Of course, you should be able to determine if she's just running from the atmosphere because she's spoiled or unaccustomed to the structure. Remember your child is responding to spending the entire day talking, playing, and interacting with other children all day, perhaps for the first time. She may need some time to adjust. Also instill in her that change is inevitable. She can't run every time she doesn't agree with something or dislikes it. We must learn to adjust. That's a part of learning.

When your child shares stories about her day with you, she may be trying to tell you about something that could be harmful to her in the long run. Because she's too young to recognize it, she may not be aware of the danger. Listen carefully to what she says when you ask, "How was your day at school?"

If you're ever stumped about how to find out what's going on in a classroom, always speak with the teacher, sit in the classroom and assist or observe for a day or two, and most important, listen to your child. Don't give up until you understand what's going on.

Some parents are concerned about the racial makeup of any classroom their children are in. I have never been concerned about my children mingling with other races. As minorities in America, they will both need to adapt to being around other cultures easily. They don't have a choice, and in fact, interacting with people of different cultures is a valuable skill for children of all races to learn. However, if your child is the only student of her race in the classroom, or one of just a few, pay special attention to how the other children interact with her, how the teacher treats her, how issues of race and culture are dealt with in the classroom, and how race is dealt with in the classroom curriculum.

Young black boys are especially vulnerable to being mislabeled as behavior problems, misdiagnosed with learning disabilities, or unfairly punished for behavior that's overlooked in other children, so be aware of this risk and respond accordingly. When in a majority setting, children from minority cultures also risk losing their own identity when they don't see anyone else like themselves. Make sure your child is constantly learning about who he is and takes pride in his culture.

Overall, you want to look for a healthy, safe, and effective environment, which is a school and a classroom where your child can be motivated to achieve the goals of the educator, goals that are in alignment with your own goals for your child's education.

Reading

So many parents are unaware of their child's reading level. Don't be one of them.

Children typically start to learn to read in kindergarten. It is your job as a parent or guardian to make sure your child continues to read and is reading at or above grade level throughout the rest of his educational career. This standard can be more easily maintained if you make sure your child also reads during his leisure hours. Find out what you child is interested in and buy books or borrow books from the library to expose him to reading about that subject. Make reading a fun experience, and read aloud with him so he can hear you read books that are more difficult with fluency. Make sure your child reads aloud to you too. That way you can identify any issues he has, and you can help him develop his reading skills. If you struggle with reading, ask someone close to your child to read to him from time to time. (In that case, I would advise you to get help with your reading skills as well. It's never too late to learn something new.)

Reading is the basic skill that makes it easier for anyone to succeed in life. It levels the playing field because anyone, regardless of race, socioeconomic background, or family background, can access the information in a book or on the internet with the power of reading. Without the ability to read, it's almost impossible to be productive in life. Not being able to read in your own language is like going to a country where everyone speaks the same language but you don't understand a word of it. You will often be lost. Understand what a powerful tool reading is, and make sure your child is prepared and can read and comprehend anything put in his hands. Help your child make reading a habit and not a chore.

Math

Text him to say, "I love you."

How important is math in a child's life during the grammar school years? Very. You would be surprised by how your child can and will master complicated mathematical concepts at an early age. We all know the importance of math in daily life, including simple things such as counting money, banking, and paying bills. But if introduced early enough, your child may grasp certain things that could turn out to be more difficult for her to grasp later in life. Purchase hands-on math games and computer software math games that will be fun to play while enhancing your child's ability to grasp new and more complex math concepts.

The possibilities for productive careers are limitless for those who excel in math. Currently there are STEM (Science, Technology, Engineering, and Math) or STEAM (which adds Art to the mix) programs that are recognized nationally and can provide your child with scholarships to private schools and to colleges and universities. Making sure that your child is learning math concepts and focusing on math skills early gives her an opportunity to learn and appreciate subjects that can make a difference in her life in the long run.

When You Can't Help with Schoolwork

As your child grows a little older, you may find the curriculum is entirely different from when you were in school. Depending on your school's curriculum, you may notice these changes as early as first or second grade. Your child comes home with a math assignment, and the first person he asks for help is you. This is an opportunity to bond that much more with your child, even if you don't know exactly what to do.

Ask your child what he learned in school about math, and see if he can explain any of it to you. Let him make the effort to explain to you what he's struggling with and what he thinks he should do. Your child is looking for you to be super-mom, super-dad, super-aunt, super-uncle, or super-anyone who's assisting in raising him. Once you determine that you have no clue how to help him, and it all looks like Greek to you, proudly say, "I don't know either, but let's find out together!" It's good for him to know that you don't have all the answers but are willing and able to find them. Remember that you don't need to know everything. You need to know how to find answers and get everything resolved so that your child can complete his homework successfully. That's what he should expect from you. That's all.

Jump on Google, YouTube, or your favorite educational website. Whatever you can think of to find the solution, the two of you should do it together. You may even have to get in your car to drive to a cousin's house, the library or bookstore, or a friend's house. Do what you have to do to get that homework completed.

Don't worry. Your child won't see you as the parent who can't do basic schoolwork. He won't think of you as the dumb parent. Instead, he'll look at you as the parent who made it happen, and he will be happy to finally understand the concepts of the assignment. He knows, at that moment, that he could not have gotten his work done if you hadn't taken it seriously. This gives your child higher self-esteem because he sees himself as important enough for you to take time out to help him with his homework, and it gives him a reason to want to go back to school the next day, confident in his ability to learn.

When my children were younger, they always came to me when it was homework time, and I was never ashamed to tell them when I didn't know something. I did whatever I had to do for them to get their assignment done correctly, and that's what they remember. My girls started to call me Nicole "Make Shit Happen" Petite and they still do (without saying the S word of course). They know I'm prepared to move on a dime to get things done, and you should make sure your child knows that about you too. You laid down and made this baby, and now you'll make sure he has everything he needs to go even farther and do even more in life than you have.

Study Skills

During elementary school, many children pick up on lessons pretty fast. Some may need a little assistance, but they usually won't need much help in the early years. The need for formal study skills will generally kick in during middle school and continue for the rest of your child's school years. However, some students may need to develop those skills earlier than others, and all children can benefit from learning how to study before schoolwork becomes more complicated. While the work at this level may not be particularly challenging for your child, this is good time to start teaching her some basic study skills. Unfortunately, most parents and children aren't aware that studying is not a skill that is taught in most schools, so it is something your child will have to learn at home.

Each of my daughters hit a point when their grades started to drop, and they felt as if they weren't "smart" anymore. They became a little less confident. Well, that's when we realized that they were both used to easily grasping the assignments in class, so they'd never had a reason to learn any real study skills. Their idea of studying was to just look over the assignment multiple times in hopes that the information would sink in. That never happens. Children have too many distractions that can keep them from learning.

I realized they didn't know how to study because they never had to put in that kind of effort in the lower grades. School had come easy for them. That's when I took it upon myself to teach both of my girls how to study. The grades came back up, and their confidence in their academic ability was higher than it had ever been.

After we realized what the problem was, I also had to talk to them about the word "smart." I had to take them down memory lane, back when I was in school and share with them that I was called smart in school. I explained that I was not smart in the way that most people usually think of the word. I was determined, and I studied. I explained there is really no such thing as someone being "smart" in the way they thought of it, because everyone had to study their craft. I gave them specific examples, like doctors, scientists, engineers, and attorneys. None of those professionals were born with their expertise. They had to study to master it.

Once my children grasped that concept, they developed strong study habits. Studying became second nature for them. They no longer dread it or feel like it's a waste of time. Since then, I've taught study skills classes for middle and high school students, and I've found that most students need help in this area. This kind of information is greatly needed in our school systems.

Here are a few tips to help your child learn to study:

- Have your child relate the material to music they love.
- Always ask for your child to be seated in the front of the class. There are so many distractions in a classroom. This allows the child to stay focused on the teacher.
- Use flashcards for dates, facts, and formulas that need to be memorized.
- Encourage your child to study out loud. Some children learn better that way.
- Use highlighters and sticky notes to identify the important details of a reading assignment and to prioritize material when studying for a test or quiz.
- Make up songs or find songs on the Internet to help your child master material that has to be memorized.
- Find another student your child can study with so they can discuss the material.
- Mark important dates and deadlines on a calendar reserved for school assignments.

- Set mini-goals and deadlines to break projects down into manageable pieces.
- Keep notebooks organized by subject.
- Keep backpacks clean and organized so homework doesn't get lost in there.
- Have one place in your house for your child to keep backpacks, books, projects, and other school material so no time is lost in looking for lost items.
- Have your child's favorite snack available for study times. This will give her something else to look forward to during study time.
- Start studying a week in advance for tests and exams.

Social Media (The Third Parent)

No one can deny that parenting has become more difficult because of social media. We are no longer able to fully monitor our children's engagements and interactions. Back in my day, we had a rotary phone, the television, our bikes, and the streetlights. Today, social media runs our children's lives. Children will buy popular items just to take a picture of them and post it on social media to get likes. (Well, adults do that too, but that's another book.) Young children rarely have the ability to separate real life from the image many people portray on social media, and they often try to emulate what they see.

Social media has the power to kill your child's self-esteem. Children become hypnotized by the images they see. They monitor the way their peers look and count the likes their peers receive to see who gets the most. It becomes a game that encourages our children to base their worth on material things, superficial images, and other people's opinions. It often creates a false sense that everyone else has more than your child does.

Regardless of how much you tell your child how beautiful she is, the approval of her peers may still hold more value than your compliments when she's overwhelmed by their comments. Social media encourages this kind of thinking. You must set limits on your child's social media use before you give her access to it, and keep it under control. For instance, when I allowed my oldest daughter to have social media accounts, I created her password. She knew from the beginning that I had access to what was going on and who she was communicating with online. Let your child know that you will monitor and control her social media activities. If she knows this up front, you won't have a hard time telling her what she can and cannot do. This is one of the moments you cannot, I repeat, *cannot* be your child's friend.

Make sure that when you're granting social media privileges, you have that talk with your child to let her know that her peers are often pretending to be something they are not. Also, talk to your child about cyberbullying. That kind of behavior can even lead to death because the bullies act on their threats or because they push victims to harm themselves. This is one of those moments, as a parent or guardian, when you must take time and pay attention to the people your child mingles with and the company she keeps online and in the real world.

When you ask your child about her day in school, listen to learn who has a cell phone in her class. These days, children as young as five years old carry cell phones. Sometimes it's because they live between two households. Sometimes their parents want them to have a phone in case of emergency. Sometimes it's just as result of living in a culture of privilege and entitlement. Whatever the reason, one cell phone in the classroom means that every child in that class now has access to the Internet and social media.

Many parents ask what age is appropriate for a child to have access to social media. In my home, it was thirteen; not until the middle school years. I gave my daughters access to one social media platform at a time, and I monitored them myself. Once I came to my own conclusion that they had matured with age and could handle the responsibility, I gave them more access. However, there were times when I had to take it from them because I saw their demeanor change and I knew their social media interactions were affecting their self-esteem.

Yes, I talked to my children every day, so it was easy to notice a change in their personalities, and my first instinct was that social media had something to do with it. Of course I brought the subject up and talked to them about it. I wouldn't be who I am if I didn't. In one instance, I advised my daughter that I saw her self-esteem diminishing. She cried, and I was angry, but we got through it. Now she can't get her head through the door (metaphorically speaking). She regained her self-esteem once I brought her "reality" from social media to her attention and made her acknowledge how well off she truly is in real life.

As a parent, I think the best solution is to address issues head on from the earliest age. Even though I allowed my children to have social media accounts at thirteen years old, the appropriate age for your child to be allowed social media is a decision only you can make, and it should be based on your child's maturity, honesty, and relationship with you. Those three factors are very important. Just be aware that her friends may have a social media access before she does, so even if you haven't given her permission to use it, she may be exposed to it by either logging on from her peers' social media accounts or just watching them. Make social media a part of your ongoing dialogue with your child.

Texting connects people in ways very similar to social media. This is something that needs to be monitored very early, as soon as your child or the friends in her class and social circle begin to have access to cell phones and tablets. There are children sexting—sharing sexually explicit messages and images—at the age of seven. Yes, seven years old.

Sexting among peers is an issue, but there are also adult predators lurking on social media, waiting for children, male and female, to show their vulnerability to them. There are people out in this world kidnapping little girls and boys and selling them in the sex trade. Talk to your child about the dangers of allowing people she doesn't know into her personal space in real life and on the Internet. Children and teens tend to accept all friends on social media in order to feel popular. This is a dangerous habit. Help your child develop a standard for who she will accept as a social media friend or follower. Teach her about privacy settings from her first social media access, and make sure she knows they aren't perfect. Even when her account is private, people she thinks of as friends can share her posts publicly.

Of course, if your child has a cell phone, she's probably smart enough to delete text messages she doesn't want you to see, but this is where you would have an iCloud account or similar technology and have all text messages go to that account. Here is the caveat. Tell your child that you are doing this. You don't want to model exactly what you don't want your child to do: being secretive and sneaky. If she has plans to be deceitful and use the phone unwisely, she will get caught. Trust me.

I know all of this seems like a chore, and it is, but remember, you are in it to win it. By choice, remember? When my children initially started texting, they immediately started using shorthand. I didn't think anything of it until I asked one of my children to write "Happy" on a box and she spelled it "H-A-P-P-I." Then I knew we had a problem. After that, I made her spell everything out to me when she texted me anything. If she misspelled a word or wrote something in shorthand, I wouldn't respond until she corrected it. Shorthand makes children lazy and comfortable with misspelling words because technology allows it. Make sure your child stays up on correct spelling. These tech shortcuts are a part of the "dumbing down" of our children. Bad spelling will spill over into papers for school, essays, and job applications—a setup for failure.

Many children these days also use a lot of profanity. They are getting it either from home or, more than likely, from their peers, television, movies, and music. Either way, too many young children use profanity when they're texting their friends, so make sure you are reading your child's messages and addressing any issues. You won't be able to stop it, but you can definitely talk about it with her and let her know you don't approve. Hopefully you are the person she hates to disappoint, and hopefully you are not using profanity around her. So many of us use the "I am grown" excuse as to why we can curse, which is 100 percent true, but don't be hypocritical when discussing her use of profanity. Make sure your reasoning doesn't allow her to use your words against you.

Other Influences on Your Child

In my experience, education accounts for only about 20 percent of a child's daily influence during the school day. This imbalance starts as early as second grade. The other 80 percent is sex (20 percent), exposure to drugs, which leads to peer pressure from people who use drugs (20 percent), fighting (20 percent), and music (20 percent). That means learning equates to only one fifth of your child's school day. Allow that to marinate for a second or two.

Now you know why the odds are against your child if he is a follower and he's easily distracted. Out of the list of threats to your child, negative rap music is the most destructive because it can influence your child to participate in other damaging behavior. I spoke on how earlier I would never tell a parent to try to stop her child from listening to destructive music. He will hear it eventually, so you might as well educate him in advance about what that music truly is. I recommend you make sure he understands that the music and the artists behind it are just a part of a performance. They are not real. They do not live the life they rap about. They rap about it because it sells.

Have a one-on-one conversation with your child about this music and the trouble it can and will bring to him or her peers. It's your job to reinforce what your child has learned in the classroom, but you also have to address the other things he learns at school. When your child comes home from school, talk about what he learned in the classroom before he bombards you with the fight that happened in the cafeteria or the girl who was caught having sex in the boy's bathroom. Oh yes, they are bumping and grinding and more at age 6–12. Trust me on this one. By talking with your child, he will recognize that his education is a priority in your household and that the distractions should be secondary. Social conversation may come first if your child is having an issue with those distractions like bullying. Only then shall it be entertained as the first conversation.

Let your child know what's important to you, and reward him when he gets his priorities right. Get the details about what happened when he was in class. Ask about projects. Ask if the concepts taught that day were hard and if he finally understood them. Ask if he needs any help. Ask if there are any upcoming exams so he gets a head start on studying for them. As long as your child learns early what is important to you, he will usually follow your example and want to live up to your expectations. This does not mean he won't entertain the foolishness that goes on in school because he probably will at different points; he's still a child, but your guidance should help keep him from getting off track. Never assume your child won't do something because you believe you've taught him better. Make sure he has his priorities in order.

Be aware of these distractions and listen to your child tell you about his day every day. That will allow you to know what's going on and, most importantly, help you recognize any potential problems that you may foresee before your child realizes they're on the horizon. Give him advice. If you have developed a trusting relationship at this age, your child should still welcome your advice.

Peer Pressure

Here is where it really gets tricky. During grammar school, your child is developing a sense of character (or a lack thereof). This will primarily be based on how you spoke with her, loved on her, congratulated her, and listened to her along the way as she comes to this point in her life. In fact, as children get older and adapt to their age group, their character may change, so this is important to remember for any age.

Leaders are not born, they are raised. Allow me to explain to you my reasoning for that statement. Children imitate what they see. If she watches you lead and take charge as a parent, she will more than likely learn that trait. If she watches you take orders and follow those around you, she will probably do the same. If you haven't yet taught your child a sense of pride and the ability to be happy with who she is as a person, she will tend to want to fit in with every other crowd. Make sure you teach her self-love and reinforce it at every opportunity before she reaches this stage of her life. If you don't, your child may just fall prey to peer pressure and become a follower. If you know you've fallen short in this area, then you need to get to work on it right away. Show her some positive leaders who she can follow, starting now, whether on TV or in her real life.

I have always said this about my children: if they ever end up in trouble, I'm almost sure they were either the leader of a group or they acted alone. They could never say, "My friend made me do it!" because they have demonstrated their leadership abilities in many areas of their lives, and they do not mind being alone. Guess where they picked that up from? You guessed it. Me. I am a loner and a leader. These girls have watched me lead all of their lives. That's all they know.

Some of the peer pressure can be eliminated if you keep up with your child's peers and what they are all involved in. This is simply done by open communication. In grammar school, know who your children communicate with on a daily basis. Whenever your child wants to stay the night at someone else's home, you now have a good reason to visit the home, meet the family, and chat with the parents to see what kind of lifestyle they live. If you monitor your child's friends and daily activities at this young age, she will expect you to do so as she gets older.

Extracurricular Activities

If you were spending a lot of your time engaging your mini-me in the preschool years, wait until she starts to have an interest in extracurricular activities. You will become more engaged. You should prepare for this turn of events and accept it as a part of your life. Remember, it's no longer about you. You know who you are. Your child is trying to find her niche. Let her, and most importantly, support her.

The worst thing a parent can do is fail to show up to support your child in her extracurricular activities (unless you have to work, which children tend to understand). Your absence may cause resentment to build up in your child, so make sure you leave communication open and don't lie to your child about why you can't show up for her. If you know you can't make an event because you'll be working, tell her that. Don't say you'll be there or you might be able to make it when you aren't sure or you know it's likely that you won't be there. That kind of disappointment leaves a lasting impact. The best way to win your child's heart, when it comes to attending sporting events and other activities, is to surprise her. It's better to make your child expect the worst and then give her the best than to give her false hope. Even when your child says she doesn't care if you show up for an event, your presence makes a difference for her, so make it as often as you can.

Your child may express an interest in a sport, club, or activity that you are not familiar with and you would never think would be her choice. Don't try to change her mind. Support her. If your son doesn't want to play football, it's okay. If he wants to play soccer or wrestle, let him know that's cool too. If your daughter wants to play volleyball instead of joining a cheer team, follow her lead. Let your child choose. After all is said and done, education should be the most important thing, and extracurricular activities are just extra.

Many parents get carried away with their children's participation in sports. They have dreams of college scholarships or want to relive their own childhood. However, if your child's grades are dropping and he's playing sports, he should be removed from all sports. Period. You should be raising athletic scholars, not athletes who happen to be students. Academics should always come first. A child can choose his own destiny when his education is his priority. If he chooses to fight for a spot in the pros, he must wait for someone else to grant his dream. That kind of opportunity may be dangled in front of a lot of young athletes, but most of them will never achieve it. Education is an advantage that cannot be taken away from your child. Take advantage of it. Practice developing your child's brain as you do his athletic

skills so he will be an educational force to be reckoned with. His athletic abilities may be natural. Learning is a more challenging task.

During football season here in my hometown, you can always find some of the mothers at the football field supporting their sons alone. Maybe the mother is there alone because she's giving the child's father a hard time about seeing their child, or maybe they were in a strong relationship at one time and the father has moved on since they no longer are. Whatever the reason, many of these women are the sole parent at the game for their sons.

There are some fathers around during the season, but, too often after the game is over, the child is dropped off with his mom and doesn't see his father again until the next game. Obviously, not all fathers out there behave like this, but way too many do. Their actions make it clear to their sons that sports matter more than anything else. This shows the son that sports are the priority. Not education. I can only imagine how many of the young boys out there on the field can't read at grade level. Some coaches enforce a requirement for good grades, but there are many coaches who only care about winning and will help their athletes find a way around the rules requiring a minimum grade point average.

Once a child sees that he can be praised for succeeding in sports regardless of how his grades look, why would he care about his grades or whether or not he can read a sign on a bathroom door? If a parent doesn't give a damn, then why should a child?

When your child starts to play sports, watch his character closely. His behavior may begin to change. If he becomes the star athlete, he may become egotistical, even at this young age. Stop him. This characteristic can lead to bullying, hurting the opposite sex, and other dangerous behaviors. Make sure he understands that arrogant, entitled behavior is unacceptable. Of course, this applies to both sexes. If your daughter is a star athlete, her success in sports doesn't excuse bad or irresponsible behavior either.

It may seem like age six is too early to worry about things like social media, texting, study habits, and sports, but it's never too early to give your child a strong foundation. The expectations you set during this time will make the middle school years—a time when our children face increasing academic and social challenges—a lot easier to manage. Many children who did well in grammar school get off track with the distractions of middle school, but that doesn't have to happen to your child.

LESSON 5
Middle School (Preteen Years)

You've made it to middle school. Your child typically hits this milestone between ten and twelve years of age, and this is when the hormones of both male and female set in and adolescence begins. At this age, your child may become very inquisitive about the opposite sex and interested in gossip, dating, and yes, sex, for the first time. How close you are to your child at this point will determine who he will go to when he has questions about all of these things. Make sure it's you.

Uncomfortable Questions

If you've established a bond of trust with your child, some of the questions he asks may make you uncomfortable. One day, I picked up my older daughter from middle school and she got in the backseat of the car. Whenever she was intrigued to ask me something, she always called my name a certain way. So that day, when she said, "Mama," with that particular tone of voice, I answered, "Yes, baby girl," and prepared myself for her question.

She asked me, "What does sex smell like?" I took a deep breath and gave her the scientific answer. Then I gave her the street answer, which was pretty much what you smell during and after someone has sex. Finally, I asked her what made her ask that question. My daughter explained that one of her friends told their other friend that the friend smelled like sex. Yeah, grab your pearls. My daughter was in the sixth grade at the time. She was ten years old.

Not long after that day, she walked into my bedroom after I had engaged in intimacy in the middle of the day, and she asked, "Mama, what's that smell?" I told her, "Sex." My daughter responded, "Oh! Okay, Mommy!" And that was that. Honesty is always the best policy, even when it makes you uncomfortable.

Honesty

When we lie to our children, we must understand that we give them the okay to do the same thing to us. The saying, "I would prefer you tell me the hard truth instead of a sweet lie" sounds cliché, but this is exactly the way we should think when talking with our children. We want them to know that, if nothing else, we will always tell them the truth. It's best that the truth comes from you regardless of how harsh it is. When something comes from someone they love, you can be there to comfort them if it's needed. The real world will give your child the harsh truth and laugh as the truth breaks her. Give her the truth and be there to comfort her when she needs it. Find the good from any difficult truth you have to share with her, whether it's a new beginning for her or a lesson learned. Sometimes, the only thing you can give her with the truth may be a hug and your love. The trust you build with your child when you're honest will certainly lead her to come to you when she needs help or advice, sometimes with life-changing decisions.

Handling the Transition to Middle School

This age is a time when children are the cruelest, and your child may also be trying to adjust to a new school, changing classrooms throughout the day, answering to several different teachers for the first time, and taking on a new level of responsibility for schoolwork while dealing with cruel peers. If you've laid the groundwork in elementary school, this transition will be a little easier, but it will still be filled with changes and challenges your child must manage.

Even if your child seems completely prepared for this transition, you need to pay attention to her to ensure you notice any struggles she may have because she may not want to—or know how to—tell you about them. The most prepared and balanced child can still face obstacles she didn't expect. You will be there to help her overcome them.

My children attended a private school from kindergarten to fifth grade. The faculty and staff nurtured them both, told them they loved them, kissed them (Ewwww!), and hugged them. It was an extremely sheltered environment, one that wouldn't have prepared them for the real world. I knew early on that when it was time for them to go to middle school, I was going to pull them out and put them in a public school so they would learn to mix with different personalities and how to deal with a wider variety of situations. Even if your child stays in the same private or public school system from grammar school to middle school, she will face significant changes academically and socially in the latter.

One of my daughters was called a "ho" during the first week she attended public middle school. When she got in my car and told me that, I cheered! That's the real world, and I wanted and needed my children to be able to handle situations just like that. The real world will often be harsh, and the elementary school my daughters had attended would never have prepared them for that reality. I asked my daughter how the name-calling had happened and how she responded. She informed me that she hadn't responded. She could have been lying to cover up something she didn't want me to know about, but that wasn't my main concern. The purpose of asking her that question was to ultimately teach her the proper response. Being the kind of mother that I am, I told her, "The next time someone calls you a ho, give them the correct pronunciation, tell them how to spell it, and explain what it means." She agreed, and we moved on.

I truly believe children should not be sheltered. You should make sure your child knows how the natural world will treat him while his parents love him through those experiences. Experience is always the best teacher. Sheltering a child from the world will only cause him stress when it's time for him to be on his own. An inability to deal with the real world can lead to depression and anxiety, and it can even end in suicide. I am no medical doctor, but I do recognize mental illness as I have suffered with anxiety myself. Having the skills to deal with life can often lessen your child's potential anxiety.

The transition to middle school is another opportunity to talk to your child about sexual predators, especially those who may be close to them or even in the family. I often asked my girls if anyone in the family had touched them inappropriately or if they felt uncomfortable because of the way someone in the family talked to them. Molestation usually happens close to home and goes unrecognized.[11] Left unnoticed, that kind of abuse can lead to a lifetime of suffering and an unhealthy outlook on life.

Below is a list to help prepare your child for middle school. These steps will ultimately help your child become comfortable faster and adapt more easily to her new academic environment.

- Make sure she attends orientation. This allows your child to meet new students and become familiar with the school grounds and her classrooms before class actually starts. This is a great icebreaker and can prevent a lot of stress during the first week. When your child is already familiar with her surroundings on the first day of school, she has one less challenge to deal with.

---

11 Child Sexual Abuse Facts. (n.d.). Retrieved March 02, 2017, from http://www.cachouston.org/child-sexual-abuse-facts/

- Make sure she keeps up with any summer assignments that she receives. This preparation definitely reduces frustration and anxiety during the first weeks of school. After all, the reason for school is to make good grades and be prepared for the next level.
- Continue to build your child's self-esteem with supportive words, encouragement, and recognition of her accomplishments. Middle school will be filled with constant criticism from her peers, so she will need to be confident in order to deal with the falsehoods of what beauty looks like, the importance of popularity, and other issues that children that age often focus on instead of schoolwork.

Social Media Influences

In today's society, we're all tuned in to our screens more than ever. We're constantly looking at our phones, tablets, television, and social media, including Facebook, Twitter, Snapchat, Instagram, and so many other online distractions. This obsession applies to children as much as adults, but spending most of her free time on social media, whether you allow her to or not, can and will hurt your child in the long run. Most preteens and teens generally want to be the center of positive attention when it comes to being in what they consider the right social circle. If your child is always on social media, her focus will be on the flyest outfit, flyest dance, flyest boyfriend, and flyest selfie.

You have to ask yourself what your child might be willing to do to become the next best *whatever* on social media. Some parents have no idea what their children are willing to do to get recognition from their peers. Some children resort to posting sexually explicit pictures of themselves or videos of violent or criminal behavior to try to get attention. You may feel you are giving your child the attention and recognition she needs, but allow me to burst your bubble. There is nothing like recognition from her peers. For many children, it's a given that parents are supposed to encourage their children, so they may not take that kind of approval seriously, especially if it comes off as being disingenuous because they haven't really earned it. Monitor all of your child's social media platforms and interactions and set limits for her. Whether or not she makes good choices may depend on it.

Peer pressure and low self-esteem can lead to your child following trends that will portray her as someone she is not or someone she is trying to be. The signs can be right in your face, and you not even recognize them or simply don't want to. For girls, this often plays out with dressing inappropriately to posting sexy pictures. Pay attention to how she dresses. I tell both of my children that you will be an adult a hell of lot longer than you will be a child. I advise them to milk that child role for as long as they can. With boys, peer pressure can often lead to risky behavior to impress people on social media, like playing with guns or fighting. The bottom line is that your sweet-smiling child can have an entirely different life online, and you have to monitor it.

Building Self-Esteem

Middle school is a rough period for all children. Hormone levels change, puberty kicks in, and learning to like themselves through all of those changes is a challenge. You must always know that when your child comes home from school she has faced more than schoolwork and instructions from teachers. Children are faced with ridicule from their peers, crushes on and rejection from others, and unwanted and unearned discipline and embarrassment from their teachers simply because they're trying to fit in or are dealing with issues those teachers don't recognize or understand. Some children are struggling with not eating the night before school, not being able to bathe because the water was turned off at home for nonpayment, domestic violence in the home, or losing a loved one. While those things may not apply to your child, they might apply to the student sitting next to her, and how a teacher responds to a child in need can affect the functioning of the entire classroom.

During the middle school years, it's especially important to pay attention to changes in your child's mood, attitude, or disposition. There will be times when he struggles emotionally, but you can have the ability to uplift him for the next day. Always inquire about his day and take time to listen to what he says and what he leaves out. Make sure his homework is done, and find out if he needs help. The first priority is always his education, so make sure he's confident about the assignment when it's completed. Do whatever it takes, at that moment, to get your child the help he needs for any assignment. Call family members or friends, and

If your child does not get the right answers from you, she will get the wrong answers in the streets.

take your child to them to get help if necessary. Mastering a challenging assignment will definitely build self-esteem in your child. Staying on track in middle school will also give your child the best chance to be prepared for college preparatory work in high school.

Your child needs to feel like you believe in him and will do whatever it takes for him to succeed all of the time. Being lazy in front of your child, especially when he needs you, is never an option. Your child needs to develop and maintain confidence in his ability to master his schoolwork. If he doesn't, he will venture off to do things that will distract him and others, like being a class clown or resorting to bullying. In middle school, there are plenty of things he can give his attention to besides schoolwork.

Once you've gotten that self-esteem lifted, help him to become confident in who he is. During these years, he may want to experiment with new hairstyles and new clothes, and he may have to deal with acne and a changing body all at the same time. If possible, provide him what he needs to feel good about himself. Try to encourage him to be his natural self and not follow trends to fit in.

Self-Knowledge Equals Self-Worth

It's especially important for children of this age to know who they are and where they came from, and this includes their family origin. This is especially important for black children. The only part of African American history that most schools have taught over the years is a whitewashed recounting of American slavery, and even that is slowly being removed from the history books. In some cases, the word "slaves" has even been replaced with the word "laborer" in the history books. The parents of black children, from my own experiences, are often not overly familiar with their specific family heritage, which can be difficult to track down. This lack of information can also make parents unsure about teaching their children about their culture and history. However, the more a child knows his ancestral history, the more confident he tends to become, regardless of where his family's roots are. Hopefully, you will have started this education for your child years before he reaches middle school, but if you didn't, there's still time. Start now. He is still inquisitive, and you can learn together.

If you don't know your specific family history, you can begin by talking to some of the elders in your family. Encourage your child to listen to family stories and use that information to find out more about your ancestry. If you want to go even further, you can use a DNA testing service to get specific details about your genealogy. I recommend this avenue because your last name, if you are of African descent, may lead to your ancestors' slave master's lineage, which won't give you enough of the details of your history. The information provided by genetic testing can open a completely new world that you and your child can explore together. There are plenty out there, and some may suit your needs better than others. Some of these companies may also be considered fraudulent, so be careful and do your research before you decided on a company. Once you know the country or countries of your ancestors' origin, spend some time studying the history and current events of the places where your family originated.

Understanding his culture's history and contributions to the world is incredibly important to helping your child know his true worth and take pride in who he is. At the same time, you also need to celebrate him. Never underestimate how important it is to tell your child how handsome (or beautiful), smart, talented, and loved he is. Don't assume he knows any of this, especially at an age when he's going through so many changes. You have to say it, but don't just tell him with words. Show him. Love is what love does. Hug him, teach him common sense, be open with him, spend time having fun with him, and say the words "I love you" often.

Here are a few ways you can boost your child's self-esteem every day without much effort at all.

- Say the words "I love you" like you mean what you say.

- Hug your child every day.
- Even when you think everything is okay, ask him if it is.
- Share some personal things about your past. Give him enough to know you're not perfect, but not too much to traumatize him.
- Let boys be boys. Don't force them to learn manly activities or take on adult responsibilities before their time. When they are scared, let them be scared. I personally do not like calling young boys young men until they reach the age of adulthood. It sets an expectation few can meet.
- Let girls be girls, and don't expect them to have the maturity of grown women or to take on a woman's responsibilities.
- Encourage your child, and support your child in overcoming challenges, whether it's an exam, a girl or boy they are interested in getting to know better, a speaking engagement, or a tryout for a sport or activity.
- Leave sweet, encouraging, and loving notes behind when you leave your child.
- Reward your child when he's doing well.
- Lastly, punish him when he misbehaves. At any age, punishment will only work if you communicate the "why" behind the punishment. This allows him to know you love him even more because you don't want him to fall in with the wrong crowd or make bad decisions.

Taking Advantage of Opportunities (No Regrets)

There's no time like the present to allow your child to start experimenting with what she thinks she may want to do with the rest of her life. If your child wants to play the violin, let her. If he or she wants to do ballet, let your child try it out. If your child wants to experiment with ventriloquism, give her the opportunity to try it. Don't put limits on your child's interests just because you don't understand the activity or don't share the interest.

As she grows older, your child may continue to be interested in the things she enjoyed in middle school, or she may not. Just like you, your child will grow and change over the years. Think carefully about forcing your child to continue with an activity she's grown bored with and wants to let go. If you really believe she'll regret giving it up, then you might want to require her to keep at it for a specific period of time. If, however, you can see that she's outgrown the activity, she's not likely to ever be good at it, or she has developed a deep passion for something else, it may be time to let her move on.

Opportunities that spontaneously arise are often the perfect chance for your children to start exploring things they like or may learn to like. Allowing them to act on a spur-of-the-moment interest helps children identify with who they are becoming and why. It also allows your child to have a separate identity from her close friends and classmates. This is a very positive step because it gives her a chance to discover her own preferences and to practice making independent decisions. That ability to make her own decision will ensure she won't easily be persuaded by peers to do things she doesn't want to do or knows she shouldn't do.

Don't ever look down on your child or belittle her because she chooses to do something that isn't to your liking because you don't understand it, you're afraid of it, or it seems out of reach. For example, many children are offered an opportunity to travel abroad during these middle school years. It's easy to say "no" due to expenses and all of the things going on in the world today. However, you have to take a step back and understand how such an experience can change the outlook your child has about the world for the rest of her life by opening her mind to things she'd never see otherwise. If there's a way you can make it happen for your child, then you should do your best to see to it that she takes advantage of these opportunities.

These are the times when you must get out of the way and let your child have the experiences she wants to have. These opportunities need to be taken seriously. You have to consider the ways in which she may benefit from the experiences, what lessons she might learn, and how she might grow. This is when you may need to let go of another finger. Just one more. If, for example, your child wants to run for class office, take it seriously and help her do her best to accomplish the goal at hand. This will teach her things about herself as well. Make sure she understands that losing doesn't mean she's not liked or loved by her peers. Sooner or later, she has to learn how to handle disappointment well, and preferably at an early age. Resilience is a valuable life skill. Your child must learn from experience to bounce back and be ready to try the next thing. The world will not wait on her to grieve. Teach her how to move on to the next success story.

Money Doesn't Grow on Trees

At such a young age, you can start to teach your child the value of money and how to manage it. If you mismanage money, your child will typically do the same thing unless you show him better money habits and work on correcting the error of your ways. When my daughters were younger, I didn't have much money, but I managed it properly, was able to explain the value of the dollar to them, and teach them about credit and what it says about your character. A few ways you can teach your son about the value of the dollar is making him work for an allowance, rewarding him when he has good grades and/or allowing him to open a saving account, and then matching every deposit he makes.

Your Turn to Ask the Questions

Middle school is a time of rapid development in your child's life. It's also a time when you should ask all kinds of questions, even those questions that some would consider unorthodox questions for parents to ask adolescent children. Please believe me when I say whatever question you ask, your child will have some kind of answer because she has heard about it, seen it, or experienced it. Don't be naïve, thinking that your child wouldn't dare do any of the inappropriate things you see other children doing. You will be wrong at least some of the time.

When you bring up a topic that could be sensitive or embarrassing, always give your child a minute to process a question that might seem totally random to him. You want an honest answer, but you have to be prepared to handle the truth without blowing up. Prep your child for the question because she may immediately decide to give you an untruth if you ask her about it completely unexpectedly. Work your way to the question so she can prepare herself to be honest. When you approach the subject slowly, your child will often guess the question you are about to ask and she'll be able to better prepare herself to be truthful right away, especially if your attitude is good and the environment is right. Most importantly, you must learn to control your emotions because when you blow up, she will shut down. An open exchange will allow the two of you to strengthen your bond of trust.

Here are some questions you might need to ask your middle-schooler:

- Are you having sex? (Ask about oral and anal sex.)
- Do you like girls? (Ask your daughter this too.)
- Do you like boys? (Ask your son this too.)
- Do you do drugs?
- Have you ever done drugs?
- Have you ever smoked weed?
- Do you drink?
- Have you ever had an alcoholic beverage?

- Do you have a crush on someone?
- Who is your favorite teacher?
- Are any of your teachers treating you unfairly? If so, how?
- Are you a bully?
- Are you being bullied?
- Have you ever been in a fight?
- Is there anyone you're afraid of or who has threatened you?
- Who is your best friend?
- Which of your friends drink?
- Which of your friends smoke weed or use other drugs?
- Who is smoking cigarettes at your school?
- Which of your friends are having sex?
- Do any of your friends have guns or have access to guns?
- Are any of your friends pressuring you to do something you know is wrong?
- Has anyone ever touched you inappropriately? Even a family member?
- What's the hardest part of being in middle school?

These are just a few questions you should ask your child, but not all at one time and not too randomly. Try to fit them in during conversations that may inspire a few of these questions at a time. Let your child know you are serious when you ask these questions, but also assure her that there will be no punishment for telling the truth—and stick to that promise. These conversations are meant to help the two of you solve any problems that may already exist and head off any bad choices she might make in the future.

If you're thinking middle school is too early to ask these questions, you need a reality check right now. In fact, you're past due for one. Hopefully your child isn't engaged in any of these behaviors at such a young age, but other children in her school or in her social circle probably are.[12] By starting the conversation with your child, you let her know that you're not naive and that you're fully aware that some children her age are already drinking, smoking, using drugs, and having sex. Your awareness can serve to give her second thoughts about doing some of those things herself.

Listening vs. Hearing

Whenever I speak with children, I ask them if they are listening to me or if they hear me, and then I ask, "What is the difference?" Children need to understand how to really listen, and your child needs to learn this skill from you. The best thing a parent or any adult can do when engaging with a child is to listen.

While you are asking questions, make sure you really listen to your child's responses. Don't just get an answer from your child and explode because you don't like what she said. If the answer isn't what you wanted to hear and gives you reason for concern, you need to ask follow-up questions.

---

12   University of Texas Health Science Center at Houston. (2009, April 10). Middle School Youth As Young As 12 Engaging In Risky Sexual Activity. *ScienceDaily*. Retrieved March 14, 2017 from www.sciencedaily.com/releases/2009/04/090408145354.htm

There will always be a "why" behind what she does. So ask why, but make sure you actually listen to the explanation. Engage in deep conversations with your child. There is a true distinction between listening and hearing. We hear noise, like the dialogue on TV, the microwave running, the birds chirping, and children playing in the background of our lives. Listening requires comprehending what you hear. Make sure any child you are speaking with, especially your own child, understands the difference and knows you're willing to listen, not just hear. Once a child knows that he has your undivided attention, he will more than likely continue to confide in you instead of always turning to his peers. Don't listen to respond. Listen to love.

Don't Let Them Shut You Out

In the midst of a disagreement or when you're dealing with an angry child, understand that the emotion the child is trying to show you is hurt. One way to control such a confrontation is to allow the child to get out what he needs to say. Once he has finished his statement, advise him to tone his attitude down because you cannot have a conversation with him screaming and shouting. Nip it in the bud immediately. The middle of a heated discussion isn't the best time to argue about who is the adult and who isn't.

We all have breaking points, even children. Many times when they lash out, it has nothing to do with trying to be disrespectful. They are truly hurting from things that they haven't been able to openly express to anyone, and you're on the receiving end of all of the anger and hurt at once. This is a time to listen and not shout back at your child. Trying to outtalk him resolves nothing. Sometimes the child could be right. Parents aren't perfect, so there could be something that you did wrong. Listen carefully, and be aware of any part you may have played in this conflict. It's better to have a conversation about how your child can constructively express his anger to you when everyone is in happier spirits. When you make a child hide his true feelings, he'll start to shut you out. When he knows he can honestly share his emotions with you, he'll do just that.

Substance Abuse

Since you are regularly asking your child important questions, there may come a day when your child reveals that, yes, she has done drugs. She may try to downplay it or act like it's no big deal, especially when it comes to marijuana use, but her honest answer gives you an open door to help her. Don't give your child the third degree. She will expect that from an adult, and she will shut down on you. Try to make her comfortable before you ask any questions. Let her know that you want to understand why she's making this choice.

Take a deep, silent breath, and calmly ask her the questions you need answered. Who have you used or smoked it with? Are they habitual drug users? Are they doing well in school? Are they even in school? How old are they? You must remain calm throughout this conversation. After all, the desired result is to find out what needs to be done to correct the issue. As my mom likes to say, you get more with sugar than salt. After you have gotten the information you need, give your child an opportunity to express and explain herself without feeling as if she's being judged.

With every word you say, she must feel as if you have her back and you love her. No judging at all. You may even have a story about how you did a little marijuana growing up, what you learned from that mistake, and why you chose to stop doing it. This may be the time to let her know that you were not perfect and you aren't judging her, but you also had sense enough to know you couldn't continue with that behavior.

After you've made your point, the two of you should do research on various drugs and learn the truth together. At the end of the discussion, your child must know you're doing all of this because you love her and want the best for her. She must also know you expect her to make better choices with the information she has now. It is true that when you know better, you *should* do better.

If you do not get the responses that you need and your child ends up being defensive and argumentative, then you have accomplished nothing. In that case, it may be more than marijuana that you're dealing with. If your child becomes very upset during the conversation, allow her to calm down. If you're busy trying to prove to her that you are the adult and control the conversation, you won't get very far. Once she has calmed down, bring up the subject again. Eventually she will talk to you or try to leave. Prepare for the worse, and know what you will do immediately if this happens. If you can't make any progress with her on the subject, get professional help for your child and for your family.

You can't always expect to get a truthful answer from your child about drug use, especially if you haven't had candid conversations about such things in the past. Regardless of how open your relationship is or how well the two of you communicate, you need to know what to look for to determine if your child could be using drugs.

Here are a few signs that your child may be doing drugs:

- Bloodshot eyes
- Unusual scents on her person or her belongings
- Overuse of air fresheners, mouthwash, and perfumes to cover odors
- Social media pictures portraying drug use
- Social media pictures portraying out-of-character behavior
- Social media videos depicting drug use or risky behavior
- Social media posts about drugs
- Cigarillos in your child's room, purse, or backpack, or the car of an older child
- Other drug paraphernalia, like rolling papers, prescription bottles, or other medicine bottles
- Dilated pupils
- Runny nose or nosebleeds
- Burned lips or fingers
- Track marks

- Extreme changes in behavior or demeanor
- A change in speech patterns, such as slurred or very fast speech
- Failing grades or a lack of motivation
- Significant weight loss or weigh gain
- Sneakiness and lying about her whereabouts
- An abrupt change in your child's social circle
- Sleeping a lot
- Any of these signs in your child's friends

These are a few of the signs that your child may be abusing drugs. And yes, this behavior often starts in middle school. Once you have confirmed that your baby is engaging in drug activity, what do you do? First, stay calm. Remember, she expects you to panic. Nevertheless, you must be willing to go to extremes from the time you find out until the time you have saved your child from herself. If you are there to embrace her in the beginning and lovingly offer her a solution, she will recognize that you have her best interests at heart. She may not say it, but she will notice that you are on her side. Of course, rehab is an option, but only introduce it into the conversation if your child is using a seriously dangerous drug or has a serious habit. In such a case, try to get your child to admit that she's addicted. This makes it easier for you to introduce rehab if it is needed.

Start spending more time with your child, even if you have to take a few days off work. This is the time to do it. I don't mean just being at home with her and sharing the space.

You need to engage in conversation with her, eat with her, and watch TV with her. Nothing should be more important than your child, so prioritize her wellbeing. It's always better to take time off to give your child your undivided attention than to take off from work to bury her. You must know that if you continue to put this issue on the back burner, your child will continue to do drugs and may engage in additional risky behaviors, such as unprotected sex, harder drugs, shared needles, and criminal activity to finance a drug habit. If you take all of the potential risks into consideration, maybe you will fight hard to save her before it's too late. Depending on the reasons behind the drug use, your child may need counseling from an expert in the area.

Whatever you decide to do to get her help, make sure she knows it's because you love her, not because she's a nuisance to you or because you want to punish her. Do not degrade or belittle her in the process. Be a cheerleader. Pull her from school and homeschool her if you must. Be upfront about the decisions you're making and why you're making them. You shouldn't do anything behind her back, like confronting her friends. That kind of response will cause her to lose trust in you and rebel even more. If the first thing you try doesn't work and your child continues to use drugs, don't give up. Continue to try every option at your disposal.

Relationships and Sex

Okay, you asked the big question about your child having sex and he boldly told you that, yes, he is. Maybe he even said it with a big smile on his face. Or perhaps you've found some evidence that your child is sexually active. Now that you have the answer you didn't want, use this time to converse with him and tell him the truth about sex.

The first thing you need to ask is whether or not he used protection. (If you have a daughter, you absolutely must take her to the doctor for a checkup, and this must continue every year for the rest of her life now that she is engaging in sexual activity. If you have a son, make sure his annual physicals include not only checking his heart, mind, and stomach, but his penis too.) Make the conversation as comfortable as possible. Not for you, for your child. You want your child to feel free to ask you as many questions as he can think of to ask. Know that if he doesn't get the right answers from you, he will get the wrong answers in the streets.

If you are a socially conservative parent, have someone who is not so conservative speak with your child. "Why?" you may ask. What your child has already heard about sex, and may have already done, is not conservative in any way, shape, or form. Having sex at this age is at the opposite end of the spectrum. Your child needs the raw truth, and you shouldn't sugarcoat it. If he ends up in a bad situation, such as contracting an incurable sexually transmitted disease like herpes or even HIV/AIDS, the world will be harsh. Even a curable STD can have long-term consequences if not treated fully and quickly. It's better to tell the harsh truth than for your child to have to live it because you didn't give him enough information. Be honest. He may already know much of this, but he doesn't have the maturity to act responsibly yet, and hearing it from you will make it harder for him to deny reality.

Show your child pictures of what STDs look like on the genitals of both boys and girls. As I've shared already, I told my oldest daughter that if she isn't comfortable enough to turn the lights on and stare at the penis up close and personal, then she shouldn't be comfortable enough to put it in her body. And I meant that. I know you can't determine if a person has an STD just by looking at the genitals, but it's a start. My daughter also knows that regardless of what she sees or doesn't see, she still must make sure her partner wears protection. I have advised my daughters that if a man doesn't initiate the use of protection, get up and run. It's safe to make an assumption that if he doesn't suggest it with you, he probably doesn't wear protection with anyone he engages in sexual intercourse with unless they make him. That's horrible. Move on from him.

I have also advised my daughter to know how to put on a condom so she can make sure that her partner has it on correctly. I wouldn't be surprised to learn that many young males often place a condom on incorrectly simply because they've bought the incorrect size. Your son or daughter needs to know that it's important to make sure the protection is on appropriately before any sexual activity starts. To your child, this may sound like something that changes the mood. But so be it! Your child's life depends on it. And that moment will probably last no more than fifteen minutes. If an adolescent child doesn't have the maturity to get through that process (which middle-schoolers certainly do not), then he shouldn't be having sex.

Teach your child that before it gets to the bedroom (I would hope it is a bedroom and not a car, bathroom, or someplace outside), he and his partner should have a full conversation about sex and what their standards and expectations are. If they can't have an open discussion about sex before they encounter it, they definitely do not need to engage in it. One of the first questions I have taught my daughters to ask a potential mate is whether or not he knows his HIV/AIDS status. That is a very bold question to ask, but sex is a bold step to take. They should be able to easily discuss the topic if both parties are prepared to be physically intimate. If this potential partner isn't open to discussing it, that reluctance should be the only red flag your child needs to walk away.

The importance of this kind of open communication can't be overstated for those of us raising African American children. According to the CDC, African Americans are more severely impacted by HIV than any other racial and ethnic group in the United States. Compared with other races and ethnicities, African Americans account for a higher proportion of new HIV diagnoses, those living with HIV, and those ever diagnosed with AIDS.[13] This doesn't mean other ethnicities are safer, but it does mean that our community

---

13   HIV Among African Americans. (2017, February 22). Retrieved March 02, 2017, from https://www.cdc.gov/hiv/group/racialethnic/africanamericans/index.html

has some work to do. This disease does not discriminate based on race. Everyone is vulnerable to catch it. Talking about this topic in detail with a sixth or seventh grader may seem premature, but remember that this is a case when you have asked your middle-schooler if he is having sex, and he has proudly told you yes. He needs this information now.

You don't have to encourage your child to talk about previous sex partners when engaging in conversation with a potential significant other or sex partner. It truly is irrelevant. That partner can have had 100 sex partners and be disease and baby-free. She could also have had one sex partner and have all of the STDs in the world or have a baby on the way. It's all in how she takes care of herself. If you are willing to have the necessary conversations, your child will learn to take care of himself and not put his desires or his partner's desires in front of their health. It's dangerous to assume a potential partner is "clean" because he or she hasn't had sex with many other people. That false sense of security could encourage your child to take risks without protection. It only takes one person to change his life for the worse.

Make sure your child develops a habit of asking the questions that could save his life. If your child isn't open to doing that, he is truly too young and immature to be engaging in any kind sexual activity. There are young girls who engage in oral and anal sex and feel that isn't really sex because it doesn't involve vaginal intercourse. When you ask your child about having sex, make sure that you include oral and anal sex as forms of sex, and explain the dangers that come with those activities as well. At this age, children tend to find themselves in relationships that never last long. Because they don't have the maturity to see the temporary nature, they consummate the relationship by having sex with the person they call their boyfriend or girlfriend at the moment. Some girls will have sex with boys to hold on to a boyfriend because boys tend to move from one relationship to another more quickly than girls do.

When my daughters started talking about boys and who liked them, we talked about sex because I recognized that many boys are finding out what it feels like to masturbate at this age, and they want to feel that same pleasure any chance they get. Many adolescent boys tend to bypass their parents and discuss sex among their peers instead. My girls know that if a boy decides he wants either of them to be his girlfriend and she thinks she wants him as her boyfriend, she should let him know up front that sex is not an option. If he decides to walk away, she can throw up her deuces and let him keep it moving because that's her signal that sex was all he really wanted from her.

I explained to my daughters that a boy with values will respect a girl more after she tells him no. The same goes for girls who demand sex from boys. Any boy who feels pressured by a girl to become sexually active before he's ready should allow her to move on. Young boys should have the confidence and self-esteem to say no just as a young girl should.

I didn't allow my children to even consider having a boyfriend until their freshman year in high school. Even then, I told them not to take the relationship too seriously so they would be prepared for the fact that it wouldn't last. I did not allow them to go to the freshman prom. I was once a freshman, and even though my mom allowed me to go to my freshman prom, I chose not to go. I already knew what most boys would expect of me that night. Wasn't going to happen. So of course I know what's going on with today's youth. So nope. Neither of my girls were allowed to go.

One of my daughter's "boyfriends" lasted all of four hours because he wanted to have sex with her as soon as they made the relationship official. Yes, she told me about it, and we both threw up the "fuck you" fingers as she said good-bye to that relationship. Coach your sons and daughters through relationships, and allow them to mingle and meet their peers so they can deal with different relationship situations while they're still under your roof and your leadership.

When my daughter decides to tell me she is monogamous, that's when I will start to worry. As of right now, she is the coach, and she recruits her team of players and kicks them off her team whenever she so chooses. She learns something from each player and moves on without being intimate with any of them.

All of this information still applies once your child is in high school or even off to college. Of course, in the best-case scenario, your child will be at least that old before he becomes involved in any sexual activity. Middle-school children are too immature to handle such responsibility. Unfortunately, the reality is that there are children in this age group who are sexually active, and you don't do your child any favors if you bury your head in the sand. The conversations that you begin at this early age should continue in the coming years. I had a conversation with a few high school students as old as sixteen and seventeen years old, and they had never heard of meningitis or mononucleosis. These two diseases start with a simple kiss. These children are still not safe when they think kissing is okay.

You may discover that your daughter has taken a liking to females or your son to males. How do you handle this? Remember that this is your child. Deciding to come out with information like that could already be stressful for him or her, and any child would want and need a parent's love and support during such a difficult time. If your relationship with your son is as strong as it should be, embracing his or her sexual preference should be fairly easy for you. Support your son or daughter. Don't be selfish. This isn't about you, your desire to have grandchildren one day, or your vision for your child's life. Your child has to live a life that will make him or her happy.

Body Language

While some children will begin to develop earlier than others, it's very clear that in today's society, girls and boys are developing much faster than many of us did when we were younger. Many theories blame the food we eat today. The FDA currently allows six hormones in the food supply, including estradiol, estriol, testosterone, and progesterone. These sex hormones can accelerate the age at which puberty occurs.[14] Whatever the cause, children's bodies are developing faster than their brains. The moment you see that your child is developing physically, it's time to start having conversations about those changes.

I can guarantee you that if you notice your daughter's breasts growing, so do the boys, and they are telling her that they see them. If your son is spending more time than ever in the bathroom, he's not shitting, shaving, and showering that long. He's probably not building a bomb either, even though you do need to make sure he isn't hiding anything like that. He's more likely exploring his sexuality. Don't rule anything out. Pay attention. All of these changes in your child are important and should not go unnoticed or undiscussed. You have to address them, or your child will get her curiosity satisfied by her peers and those answers will not be the ones you want her to hear.

Social Media and Cyberbullying

I want to elaborate on the pitfalls of social media and dangers of cyberbullying because, unless you are a very young parent, you didn't have to deal with these things as a child. This topic is very important, and if parents don't give it the attention it deserves, it can lead to the suffering, depression, or even death of your child or someone else's child.

If you have a child who is a follower by nature, social media may not be the best thing for her. While you can work

---

14 http://www.foxnews.com/health/2012/10/05/hidden-hormones-can-bring-about-early-puberty-in-kids.html

with her to develop her independence and her leadership skills, social media can be a dangerous place to test her. This is why it's very important to be the go-to person in your child's life. If you aren't, social media can begin to define your child's values and provide validation for her. Nothing good can come of that.

If you're paying enough attention to your child, you will notice any personality changes she starts to display. This can include a sudden drop in her self-esteem or starting to hang out with a crowd that seems to enjoy bullying other kids. If your child hangs with bullies and doesn't do any bullying but stands by and watches, she is guilty by association, and you need to let her know that. In this case, your child needs new friends. Those types of peers are not friends to begin with and can just as easily turn on her. This kind of bullying often happens online, through social media, because children find it easier to hide cyberbullying from adults.

You must be a parent who's up on technology and social media at all times. You should be able to log on to your child's social media accounts and see what she has going on at any time. This way, you can see who she's portraying herself to be. Unchecked access to social media can be dangerous for her. Your child could be "beefing" with someone online, and that can lead to violence in real life. You need to know. She will probably not tell you about it, so make this an important part of your daily routine. It could save your child's or another child's life. I've confronted a few boys, girls, and parents about my child's interaction with another child on

How's Your Mental?

A question that we very seldom ask our children when they wake up or when they come home from school, work, etc. This is a question I have asked my girls since they were young enough to comprehend what I mean when I ask them this question. I still ask both of them this question this day. Why? As I have stated in a previous lesson, our children are bombarded with images and actions as they head to school, to work, or wherever their venture may be for the day. What are you as a parent doing to stimulate their emotions to be positive? Are you yelling at her to rush and catch the bus every morning? Are you providing him with soft spoken love and some breakfast to feed his mind before going off to pass those exams? A parent is usually the first adult the child encounters in the morning and the last when they come home. Are you her safe space? Are you fussing and yelling when he comes in the house? Do you ask, "How's your mental?" or "How was your day?" Are you really interested in hearing her express herself about any trauma the day caused? Especially if you caused it. Are you showing excitement if he comes home and wants to tell you about some exciting news that happened that day? Are you truly listening? I have learned that when I child is given a space to speak freely, she will. You can hear depression, anxiety, fear, excitement, etc. all in the 10 mins you give him to speak to you about their day. You discover what worries him, his grades, and even how he feels about his teachers. This is the time to try to solve those obstacles and help your child succeed more. We have way too often shunned mental health as "oh he's just crazy" when the entire time they have suffered trauma from Uncle Joe or Aunt Jane assaulting them, or she may need glasses as to why she is not doing well in school simply because they can't see, or he's being bullied and contemplating suicide and no one knows because no one asks. The biggest bully could also be the parent. Is this you? Ponder on these questions before answering defensively. Having these hard conversations with your children allows them to open up and propels them to become better humans. They learn how to manage their stresses and not just cope with them. They learn to be expressive without fear.

Children deal with trauma in different ways. Some children attach themselves to loved ones and those that appear to be loved ones while others may remove themselves from these very same loved ones. Some become angry and short tempered while others become more emotional. I have learned how I traumatized my girls after the fact. My oldest, who is a grown woman now, still hears me walking to her bedroom to fuss because her room was not cleaned. My youngest remembers me fussing because she didn't complete a task. They were both effected by death and other situations in their lives that may have altered their personalities. I was not afraid to immediately offer more therapy, love, openness, and hugs. I became more of a punching bag and sounding board for my girls to have that safe space to exhale and release anger, sadness, and even express their love for me.

I want to bring up eustress. According to Merriam Webster, "eustress is a positive form of stress having a beneficial effect on health, motivation, performance, and emotional well-being"1. This type of stress is warranted and if stress is given, this should be the first form of stress in the morning. This will motivate them to achieve a goal before the day is over. A positive goal. Something that will enhance their future dreams.

So, parents, make sure upon waking up in the morning, you are soft speaking, loving, kind, encouraging, and caring to your children before waking them up with rage, rush, unconcern, and an unloving environment. Help them start their day off with positivity, high self-esteem, and a willingness to want to go out in the harsh environments of the world and learn something besides what is thrown in their faces all day long through social media and social engagement with peers. They see and hear everything. Allow them to come home to a safe space of love and an anxiety-free environment.

---

1 Merriam Webster <https://www.merriam-webster.com/>

Struggle Loving Your Children

As I became a parent, I started to hear other parents talk about how they wanted their children to go through some type of suffrage to determine if they were ready to be out in the world and be able to withstand the harshness that comes with it. In their minds, they believed that going through struggle made them understand life and the pursuits of it all. To me, it shows that the parent only knows a life of struggle and wants the child to go through life the same way. On purpose. As if there is no other way to live. As if the child cannot live a life without much struggle. Isn't that the purpose? To ensure them a better life than we had as parents? When we do this as parents, what is your mindset for them to accomplish struggle? Are you forcing your child to sell drugs, walk miles to and from school, take punches from a fight, defend a parent while being robbed, work a full-time job while trying to go to grade school all while doing all of this as a child? One parent's struggle for a child can look completely different from the way another parent wants their child to struggle to succeed. Ponder on this for a second. Whose future life is this making better? Where did this come from? Why do you feel a child has to go through more trauma to gain respect or make the child believe they have to "get it out the mud" because you had to? What does that do for you as the parent? What rites of passage do you feel that child has gone through once they "get it out the mud" based on what that means to only you? The bigger question is, what is it doing to your child mentally? Will they carry on this generational "tradition" or "curse" to their children? The entire purpose of our ancestors going through what they have gone through was for us to not have to go through it. It should get better for each generation. My ancestors literally fought and died for the basics. My mom struggled to make sure I lived a better life than she did and gave me the peace I needed as a child to focus on what children should focus on. She did this for me to have a better life for myself. And in return, I have done the same for my children. I want us to try and discern between how to uplift our children out of love and how watching them struggling to make them tougher effects them, whether negatively or positively. Some struggles can be lessons, but should they be traumatizing to the mental? No. If we teach them what struggle is, they should not have to go through it because our ancestors, our parents, and quite a few of us have already gone through the struggle for them. Let us eliminate as much stress as possible to make room for mentally positive children growing into adults, making room for the child to focus on things that they will succeed in and not be concerned about an unwarranted struggle.

Making decisions that could do harm to our children's mental is something we may be doing without even realizing it. In these moments, if we can stop and think about our actions and try to realize how the decisions and pressure, we put on our children at such young ages affect them for the rest of their lives mentally.

Mental Check in During and After Marriage

So many children, including mine, experience divorce and are able to clearly verbalize what they are seeing, how it is affecting them, and how it affects their future. But no one ever asks, "How is your mental?" In fact, a lot of children are thrown into the middle of divorces as the referees and the punching bags, and it is more than they can handle and should not handle as young children. As a divorcee, my children and I went through therapy. I also made sure my girls were as happy as that event could allow them to be. Their emotions and mental state mattered just as much as mine did. So, I made the necessary sacrifices to make sure they were in the best head space they could be. So, parents, try and consider the babies when going through the divorce and realize that you do not go through it alone. The children go through it with you.

As we continue to grow with our children, as long as you continue to love them PROPERLY, they will become kind, productive, and loving adults in society and that alone should be a job well done to you and the child.

social media. The problem ended quickly because I addressed it. The young children said I was "tweet watching." Well at least they knew I had my eyes on them.

Opening Their Minds to Career Options

Through all of the turmoil your little one faces in middle school, you still must have a clue about the career direction your child is headed in when he reaches adulthood. Yes, if you haven't already, now is the time to start having that conversation.

You don't have to have a formal talk with him. You just want to guide him, and help him start making some distinctions and acknowledging his own preferences and strengths. Ask him what subjects he thinks he excels in at school and which subjects he enjoys the most.

This is not the time to come out and tell your child he must choose a career and stick with that choice for the rest of his life. Don't do that. Just play around with the idea of what he sees himself doing in the future. Discuss the different career options related to the things he enjoys doing and learning. A lot of children have a dream career in their minds as early as five years old, so the topic shouldn't be completely new in your household. Of course their choices may change drastically as they get older.

Some parents like to tell their children that it doesn't matter how much money they make when they pick a career, and what matters is that they enjoy their career/job. Well, "I can't pay my power bill but I love my career," said no one, ever. Give your child salary information for different careers so he can plan to start building wealth early in his career. Help him to choose a path that will let him earn a great living while doing work he enjoys.

Middle school is also the time to start prepping your child for standardized testing that can earn him scholarship opportunities, some of which may include full-ride academic college scholarships. Have your child take the ACT and SAT at least once a year, every year, beginning in the eighth grade. It can only enhance his chances of scoring high and being rewarded for that success. If he needs a prep class, help him find one. There are free courses available online and prep books available at the library, so there's no longer any reason for any child to show up unprepared for a standardized test.

The middle school years are often the most stressful for children because they're caught between their childhood and their teenage years. During this time, academic demands increase and friends may change. It's a lot for them to deal with, but with your help, your child can navigate this time successfully and enter high school ready to succeed.

LESSON 6
High School (Teen Years)

Whoo! You've made it to high school. You're probably saying to yourself, "My child is more independent now, and she doesn't need me as much." You could not be more wrong. That child needs you more now than she ever has, so buckle down. At this age, your child should know more about who she is, her family history, and most importantly, her goals, dreams, and aspirations for the future she's quickly approaching. This self-knowledge builds high self-esteem. If you are just now starting to read this book and she's already in high school, go ahead and start building her self-esteem based on the tactics I suggested in the previous chapters and what I'll share in this chapter. It's never too late.

Your child should be confident and secure in herself when she's out in the world alone. This comes from the things you have instilled in her from birth, and encouraging her to believe in herself is an ongoing conversation. Like middle school, high school is also a time when your child may be susceptible to picking up bad habits from new peers as well as old peers. Parent-child communication continues to be incredibly valuable during this phase. With all the listening and conversing you have done with your child from the earliest age, there's a good chance that she will take what you've taught her on her daily life adventures.

You have instilled the difference between right and wrong in her. (I always tell my children, "All I can do is instill in you what is right and what is wrong, so I am not to blame if you go out into the world and do wrong. You knew better before you did whatever it was that put you in a compromising position.") However, even after they've learned right from wrong, things aren't always so simple. Peer pressure really does exist, and all the distractions that started in middle school only increase their demands for your child's attention in high school. Most children want to fit in somewhere, so monitoring your child is still as important today as it was when they were younger. Examine whether you taught your child to be a leader or a follower. Remember: leaders are not born; they are taught. Continue (or start) to show your child how to lead. To do that you have to lead in her presence as she gets older, or make sure she is in the presence of someone who leads constantly.

Ask your child about her day and her schoolwork when she gets home from school every single day.

Sometimes, our boys need more attention than our girls do. Too often, boys are forced to act mature too early in their lives even though we know they mature more slowly than girls do. Putting pressure on a boy to become a man before he's ready causes too much stress. In our society, a boy never really experiences a rite of passage that says he is an adult, so the line between boyhood and adulthood can be blurry. Young boys are told at too early an age that they are men. Allow them to be young, and be there for them just as much as you would be for your daughter. Most moms tend not to have a problem supporting sons because of the strong bonds they have with their boys. However, some mothers put pressure on their sons to be the leaders of the home when the father is temporarily or permanently absent, or until another man moves into the home. Forcing a child to make adult decisions and take on too much responsibility before he's ready can lead to the child making irrational decisions and possibly putting himself in harm's way.

On the other end of the spectrum, some mothers have a tendency to baby their boys, coddling them well beyond the time when they should be encouraging them to be independent. Don't fall into that trap. Just like we expect girls to take on responsibility, like cooking, helping with housework, and helping with younger siblings, we should expect boys to do the same.

During this phase your child needs your support as much as or more than ever. Ask yourself this question: "Do I usually discourage my child or try to change her mind when she tries to talk to me about something she's interested in?" This is an important question to ponder. If your child recognizes she has the support she needs from at least one adult close to her, she will move about the world comfortably and have confidence in her choices. Your child, at this age, needs to know that you are a genuinely just a phone call or text away.

Academic Progress

You must instill in your child that the main goal of high school, from day one of her freshman year, is graduation. Every choice your child makes along the way can determine whether the final outcome will be graduating, dropping out, a ride on the school-to-prison pipeline, or scholarship opportunities and a chance to go to college. This needs to be reinforced on a daily basis. Don't wait until she's a junior or senior to discuss these issues. In her freshman year, the two of you should have ongoing conversations about career opportunities, potential college and university choices (if that is her path), standardized test preparations, and military or trade school options. When she has a specific goal in mind and she's excited about her future, your child will be more likely to stay on the right path. These goals will make her think twice about mischievous actions and careless decisions during high school. Find a way to expose her to new careers and opportunities. This exposure will help see how she can get over those obstacles that may get in her way.

It's also important to be on top of your child's class schedule in high school. There are classes that can be taken that will transfer to college so that she starts her college career with some credits on her transcript. There are specific classes she must take to have a chance of being accepted at her first-choice college or any reputable four-year college program. Contact the guidance counselor before your child starts ninth grade to make sure she selects the right classes for her chosen career path.

Academics take first priority, but there is more to high-school life. Make sure your child has community service options available to her, and encourage her to serve. This will keep her busy with positive work and give her the community service hours required by some high school honor societies and many colleges and universities. Community service work can also help a child who doesn't have perfect grades qualify for college scholarships or win academic scholarships when her competition doesn't have as many community service hours. Community service is a must.

During high school, your child may also want to become more involved in extracurricular activities. This is good. It can help her meet new friends, discover new interests, and build her resume for college applications. Allow her to explore those options, but reinforce that academic success is the most important part of school. Make it clear that if her grades drop, you will have to remove her from the extracurricular activities. Make sure you keep up with her grades on a daily or weekly basis, depending on how much monitoring you know your child needs. In high school, my children had a goal of maintaining a 3.5 each quarter. If their goal wasn't met, I removed them from their extracurricular activities and took away their phones. I did this not to punish them but to allow them to focus on what was important. They both understood my actions because we had an ongoing conversation about their priorities.

The Transition to High School

Especially in the beginning, high school can be a very scary place. Your child's upbringing and many of the choices he made in middle school will determine how he'll adapt to his freshman year of high school. If you're honest with yourself, you know if your child is a leader or a follower, a loner or a child who must have friends around at all times. I have taught both of my children to allow others to attach to them, not the other way around, and I suggest you teach your child the same thing. This way, your child will not change to meet the needs of his peers. His peers will change to meet the needs of your child.

Once a child goes looking for friends, he tends to change his character to fit whoever he's following, and that is not what I wanted for my children. Because they aren't desperately seeking friends, my daughters have no problem with studying alone, walking to class alone, or eating in the cafeteria alone. They are able to move about the world alone because of the high self-esteem and their knowledge of self. Remember, it is solely up to you to start teaching that in the very beginning, or as soon as possible, to get them to this point in their lives. It is vital.

Some children may find doing things on their own difficult. They may see it as being antisocial or an outcast, but I've taught my children to recognize that having the kind of confidence that many people do not possess in adolescence or even in adulthood is a great strength. Once your child recognizes and owns his self-identity, he won't compromise who he is for anyone. Strong self-identity creates high self-esteem. Teenagers who know who they are and are comfortable with it tend to have higher self-esteem and can handle the challenges, temptations, and distractions of high school.

If your child is struggling with the transition to high school, there are a few steps you can take:

- Build his confidence by encouraging and complimenting him after school every day.
- Make sure he has what he needs to complete his daily assignments.
- Make him laugh when something is bothering him, and then offer a solution.
- Get in his business.
- Tell him you love him every day.
- Discover what he likes about school and talk about that often.
- Let him know you are there for him.

Insecurities

Insecurities can negatively affect every area of your child's life. Insecurity starts at home and must be debunked every day when you have a teenager. Social media has warped these young minds into believing what they see. Many teenagers don't realize that many images they see are photoshopped and the lifestyles many people claim to be living are fake.

So how do we correct our babies in a world full of stereotypes and expectations? You must encourage your child on a regular basis, and listen to her every day. Both of my daughters get highly upset with me if I am on the phone when I pick them up from school. They want my undivided attention. They are used to getting it, and they want nothing to get in the way of our time together. I make time for it. I get off the phone. I turn down the radio. I make sure they know they are the most important people to me and the world stops for them. I have to admit that it's kind of cute and makes me feel all warm and fuzzy inside when they pout and are upset because I'm on the phone. There have been times they have cried because they were so upset with me. They really wanted my time and attention! Hopefully, you've already established this kind of relationship with your child, but if you are just starting, don't fret. Make sure she recognizes that she has your undivided attention when you talk to her. It won't take long to create new expectations of closeness and communication if you get to work building that relationship immediately.

Build up your child's self-esteem with real praise for the things she has accomplished. Don't make the mistake of giving your child false praise. Everybody's good at something, so find what she's good at and give her praise for that. At this age, your child still needs to hear from you that she's beautiful, smart, capable, and a good person. She might act like those compliments don't matter coming from you, but they do, even as she gets older. She will remind you of those compliments when she is grown and has children of her own, and she probably will do the same to her children because she will remember how you made her feel.

You're Still in Charge

At this age, your child will be struggling to balance her need for independence with her need for you. If you see your child distancing herself from you, pull closer and get all in her business and continue to make the decisions you believe are best for her. Yes, she will be upset, but as I used to tell my oldest daughter when she wanted to go party with her peers during her senior year, "If there is a .000000001% chance that harm can be done to you, you can't go." Yes, we fought, but she realized in the end that I preferred her to be mad and alive instead of happy for a few minutes and then dead. I didn't care about her peers or what they thought when she couldn't hang out with them. Not at all.

I conversed with my daughter so she could understand why I did what I did, and I allowed her to express her feelings to me as well. I wooed her because I was able to explain to her how things were much different when I was growing up compared to now. She was happy and embraced the fact that I wasn't trying to punish her. I just wanted her alive and well. I always expressed that she wasn't a mistake, and my plan is for her to bury me, not the other way around. Moreover, that was the last conversation we had to have. She stopped asking, and even stopped having a real interest in going to those events.

The senseless deaths, random violent acts, and accidents only helped solidify my case as time went on. "I told you so'" became silent eye winks and "mm-hmms." She and I were able to giggle just a little bit with each other, and she gave me that "Okay, mama, you won" laugh. My girls recognize the love I have for them. They know a lot of their peers do not have this kind of love at home. I've told them many times, "I bet your peers would love to have have a mom who gave them the attention I give you." They both agreed, which explains why a lot of their peers were always at my home. I engaged in conversation with all of them, the kind of conversations that their parents didn't have with them.

Where many parents go wrong is that they refuse to explain their feelings, actions, or decisions to their children. If a child does not understand, she's much more likely to lash out. There is absolutely nothing wrong with giving your child your truth about why you make certain decisions for her. It doesn't make you a weak parent. It strengthens your relationship with your child. When you do something out of love for her and a desire to protect her, your child still may not like it, but she's more likely to accept it.

Of course, your child will be more receptive if the two of you already have a strong bond and regularly communicate with each other. If you are just getting involved in your child's life at this stage, it will be a little more complicated. Keep talking, keep listening, and make sure you drink your energy drinks because you will be running behind your child to keep up and stay involved. With all of that, don't allow your child to do things that you know won't enhance her life just so you can feel like her friend or simply to make her happy for the moment. That never works. Always encourage your children. Tell them they are beautiful or handsome. Hug them. Tell them you love them. Show them you love them by spending time with them—not by showering them with gifts. Your time is the most important gift you can give your children.

Engaging with Their Peers

Your child's peers play a very important role in who he is at any given moment and who he's trying to be. Teach your child to walk alone and allow his peers to flock to him. That way he will have no desire to change who he is. His peers will follow him. Get to know all of his friends. This is easy to do if you talk with your child every day and ask him how his day was. It will become natural for your child to tell you about his social activities. Pay attention to the stories he shares with you and notice who leads and who follows. You do not want your child to be the follower in any social relationships unless that arrangement benefits him in some way.

Make the Most of Summers

We typically consider summer a time for the children to unwind from school, relax a little, and, of course, have some fun in the sun. Time off is important, but what I also do for my daughters during the summer is get them a step ahead in education. They might work an internship to help them make better choices on their career path, take summer classes at a local college, do volunteer work that they will enjoy, or work a paying job. Whatever they do over the summer, I also want them to enjoy what they're doing.

Going to school in the summer may sound bad, but they also meet new people and get a feel for college, which allows them to be and feel a little more independent and mature when they officially start their college classes. An idle mind really is the devil's workshop, so make sure your child is busy being productive in the summer. There are high school and college internships that your child may qualify for and use to gain valuable experience. There are also plenty of organizations that your child can join that are quite busy during the summer, touring colleges, exploring business ventures, and helping students make good choices for the future. I currently host a club called The Six Figure Club, which allows children of all ages to come in and discuss career opportunities. We help them think about their goals for their future careers. This is the kind of organization you can easily start in your community.

While you should keep them occupied and productive, you should also plan a small vacation to give your family a chance to bond and discuss the future with your child. Be your child's biggest cheerleader. These vacations can only bring you closer together, so do what you can to make them happen. We always plan at least a weekend at a beach, because we are close to several of them, or we will take a trip to nearby New Orleans. The vacations do not have to be anything expensive. The main focus is bonding and creating memories. There is no time like the summer time to spend more time with your child, whether they are in college or high school. You both can learn from each other, and it keeps them out of the streets.

Applying to and Preparing for College

By the time your child reaches her junior year, she should be well prepared for what's to come after high school graduation. If you wait until her senior year, frankly, it will probably be too late to help her make the most of the opportunities available to her. It will definitely be harder to plan for post-educational success. If your child is planning to attend college, she should have taken the ACT, the SAT, or both at least a couple of times before her senior year. She also needs to have researched colleges and taken some college tours, maybe as a part of your summer vacations, by this point. When your child chooses a potential career path, you can help her plan for everything she'll have to do to achieve that goal. Even if her choice changes later, like after she starts college, she will have a solid foundation to build on, and she'll know how to take action to go after what she wants. Start with Google. Find out what steps are required to achieve her desired career. Also, search for someone in that field who lives near you. See if he or she will mentor your child or at least sit for an informational interview. I believe in the saying, "A closed mouth doesn't get fed." The worse response you can get is a "no," and I am okay with that. No is good for the soul.

At this stage, your child needs all the support she can get from you. She's approaching a phase of her life that she'll explore on her own and she needs to be confident that she'll be just fine.

If your child is going to college (and most of our children should be), make sure she starts the application process in the beginning of her senior year. Don't leave this up to her. Make sure you (or another trusted adult) are reading over essays and making sure deadlines are met. Some universities cut off scholarship applications in December, so applying for these opportunities early will make all the difference in the world.

Applying for financial aid by filling out school forms and the FAFSA (Free Application for Federal Student Aid) as soon as the financial aid season opens for the next school year will give your child the best possible chance to get various types of aid. Even if your child receives a full scholarship, the FAFSA must be completed. The scholarships come through this application to be applied to your account. Consult fafsa.ed.gov to find out when the next application season begins. Parents have to fill out those forms, so have your most recent tax returns ready, and get it done as soon as you can. Don't allow your child to wait until the deadline to submit applications to universities or for scholarships. These things are almost all submitted online, and because so many applicants wait until the last minute, the websites often get overloaded and crash. If your child can't get on the site, she may miss the deadline and lose out completely. Filling the FAFSA out early also offers the opportunity for her to receive a bigger Pell grant if she qualifies for one.

Ask your child's college counselor about the options for applying for early admission or early application to different schools. The Common Black Application, www.commonblackcollegeapp.com, allows a student to apply to fifty-three (and that list is growing) Historically Black Colleges and Universities, for a small fee, all at one time. I am an HBCU advocate, so I often recommend this route. Take the time to research other avenues to streamline the application process. For some students, these options will increase the chances of acceptance and make them eligible for additional grants and scholarships. It may mean doing additional work beyond the Common Application, but it will be worth it in the end. If your child's high school doesn't have effective college counseling, do what you can to get guidance. There are independent college coaches you can hire to help your child, and many nonprofit groups offer help with the college application process. You can also head to my website, NicolePetite.com, and "Ask Nicole." I will be glad to help guide you in the right direction.

Managing Money Independently

Before my older daughter went off to college, I informed her of how the credit card companies sucker students into getting credit cards by offering them free pizza, T-shirts, and other gifts to get them to sign their name on the dotted line. This is a disaster waiting to happen.

My mom allowed me to get one credit card in college, but I could not charge anything on it unless she gave me permission because she paid the bill. A lot of students don't have parents providing that type of discipline, or they get the credit cards and don't even inform their parents. And what happens? They max out the credit card on food and clothes before the semester is over, and it becomes listed as bad debt on their credit report the following month. They do this one to three times, and they end up with both student loans and bad debt credit cards on their credit when they graduate college. Not a position your child wants to be in when he's looking for a career or trying to branch out on his own and secure his own apartment and a vehicle. Teach your child the dangers of credit card solicitations before he gets to college, and inform him of the potential consequences. This is a message you'll have to repeat over and over throughout his college career.

Your child also needs to learn the importance of saving as soon as they are able to comprehend what it means to save. And even if they don't fully comprehend, if they start early with saving, it will become second nature for them to do. Hopefully, you've been teaching him this from a young age, but if you haven't, it's not too late. I didn't start saving until I was older, after I learned, for me, that it was best for me to save before I paid my bills. That's how I put myself on a budget. Once I moved the funds over into another account, it was out of sight and out of mind. Many of today's youth spend money as fast as they get it to keep up with the Joneses. Teach your child to invest or spend money on things that can increase their net worth. If your child is confident in who he is, materialistic items will not intrigue him. Use this time now, while your child is still in your home, to instill good money habits in him so he'll know how to live within his means, avoid bad debt, and build savings and investments as he goes off into the world.

Alternatives to College

I used to run a program called Takingovermyfuture.com. This program focused on exploring every post-educational opportunity there is for a student after graduating high school. Our goal was obtaining college for as many students as possible, but we all know that not everyone wants to attend college, so we shouldn't force them. That kind of pressure makes for a higher dropout rate, with students borrowing funds from the government and not putting it to good use or simply borrowing without the end goal of graduating from college or trade school. So what do you do with a child who isn't on track for college or really has no interest in higher education?

A four-year college experience isn't for everyone. Some students need more time to mature before they attempt to

go out on their own. Others have goals that don't require that they attend college right out of high school or at all, such as a military career or a particular trade that has the potential to be a lucrative career. Some students have gotten off track academically and need some time to rebuild their academic record.

If your child shows an interest in a military career, do the research together. Ask questions. Find out why he wants to go into the military and which branch appeals to him and why. Find out what his plans are for his time in the military. Does he want to spend his entire career in the military and retire from the service? Does he plan to go to college and use government funds to pay for his education? Find out what his end goal is. Make sure he is aware that written and physical tests are required for enlistment. Some students simply try to avoid tests and think the military will allow them to do that. The exams taken in the military will determine his career while he serves. This is important. Also, make sure he is aware about what's going on in the country and around the world before he makes such a huge decision. It could cost him his life.

Your child may choose to go to trade school. Be there with him to do the research and support him. There are plenty of career opportunities in that arena that lead to high paying careers and even entrepreneurship. Your goal should be to help him become a happy, productive, independent adult, whatever path might lead him there. Explore these alternatives early in the high school years as well. The earlier you know what career path your child wants to pursue, the sooner you can start finding the road to success for your child.

Many parents think that as a child enters high school and becomes more independent, the parent's job become less important. Your child may have a driver's license, honor roll grades, and a big vocabulary, but she still needs your guidance and support. As your child goes through high school, make sure she stays focused. Continue to pay close attention to behavior changes and who she's hanging out with. These years are very important to your child's future. During this time, if she hasn't already, she should develop an attitude of determination to reach her goals. Make sure the goals that have been set match her interests. If you, the parent, has set all the goals for your child, the chances of your child following those goals are slim. That's a recipe for rebellion.

The high school years probably look like they'll be a lot of work for you as a parent, and that's because they will be. Remember, you signed up for this journey when you had your baby, and you need to see it through to the end—and there's no real end. Even after you get your child through high school and headed in the direction of his life goals, he'll still require your love, guidance, support, and encouragement. That's why it pays to be prepared for college and beyond.

LESSON 7
College and Beyond

If you have made it this far with your child, congratulations! Now is the time to pat yourself on the back. I don't give credit to any parent for making sure a child graduates high school. That's what they are supposed to do. That's the minimum. That's just like giving me credit for being a good mom. That's my job. The real celebrating comes after your child walks across the stage and begins the practical steps to reach his career. Don't relax yet. This time in your child's life can be scary for both of you, whether you're sending him away from home or preparing him to take more responsibility for himself while still living at home for a while.

If your child is going away to college, make sure he isn't going to a school just to say he went. He needs to understand that he's going to school to graduate into a career. College is not a career; it's a launching pad to the future. There are far too many students who attend a university because it's the popular choice, only to discover the university doesn't even have the major they plan to study.

Your child's choice of college isn't necessarily permanent. He can always transfer if it's necessary, but that can affect any scholarships and other financial aid he's been awarded. It's best to do all you can to ensure that he makes the best choice for himself in the first place. Even though your child should have an idea of what he wants to study when he gets to college, people do change. Don't get upset with him if he decides to change his major. Many college freshmen have no idea what they want to do. If they do, it's because they started exploring their interests early. Sometimes they get burned out on a topic before they actually start to study, depending on what they were doing before they got to college. Activities such as internships, community service, or work in that field may show them that the path they thought was right isn't really right for them.

Take a deep breath, and allow your child to make these decisions for his future while you give him your full support. Part of being independent is making decisions for himself and feeling confident about the decisions he makes. Be there. That's it. The most important and effective things you can do as a parent, while your child is in college, are support him, encourage him, and love him every step of the way. If he asks your opinion, give it to him. If you think the decision he is about to make may harm him, ask him if he's willing to listen to your

> Tell your child "no" sometimes because the world will tell him "hell no." Teach him to brush off rejection and move on looking for the next yes.

opinion. Let him know that he still has to make the decision on his own, even after he hears your advice, unless it's a very detrimental decision. In that case, you'll have to do what you can to step in and require him to make a different choice. Your support will carry him through to graduation. The lack of that support may lead to him dropping out before he finishes his degree.

Sometimes I send my daughter, who is now in a pre-med program, flowers—just because. I also remind her that the real "turn up" time is not homecoming or a random party on the weekend, even though I understand that she will "turn up" at these events too. The real "turn up" time is when she passes a test. As a reward, I will treat her to pizza delivery or something nice to make her feel as if she has accomplished something important. (It usually ends up with me buying her clothes.) Nothing big. Just small rewards to celebrate her milestones. She needs those small rewards to help motivate her to get to graduation for the big award—her degree. Continue to motivate your child and let him know you are proud of him, even when he doesn't feel proud of himself. That support goes farther than you can imagine.

While your child attends college, you still need to be involved with him to help make sure he stays on track to maintain the GPA he needs to keep his scholarships or simply to graduate. During college, we, as parents, do not have access to our children's grades unless they sign the proper paperwork. Encourage your child to give you that permission but also to share his progress and his struggles. Reward him when he does well. It's hard to try to manage a child's whereabouts or actions while they are in college, so you have to accept that, for the most part, you won't be able to control or know everywhere he goes. However, you can still inquire about his grades and ask if he needs help. Make sure he knows that you are there to support and not chastise him.

One thing I know for sure is that, as a parent, you need to make sure you support your child whether he's away at school or in training or in town with you. You need to be especially supportive when your child is away from home. My daughter was not the happiest child during her first year in college. She became sad and depressed, and she wanted to come home. I could have told her she couldn't come home, to "suck it up" and get through it. That's what a lot of parents do, thinking that is making their child stronger. Some children are able to get through things that way, but that was not how I wanted to support my child.

I let my daughter know I was here for her, and I drove to the university and picked up my child almost every weekend. I brought her home so she could have some peace of mind and to be able to lay in her own bed and mingle with her family, as often as possible. That allowed her to keep her sanity and keep her grades up, and she renewed her faith that no matter what, her mom will always be there to support her. Doing anything less might have caused her grades to fall, resulting in losing her scholarship and ending up back at home.

Please don't allow your child to be left out on his own when he is most vulnerable. You may not have the luxury of picking up your child the way I did. He may attend a university that's too far away for you to go and get him or even visit him often. Do whatever you can to make him feel secure in your love and to make sure he knows you have his back. Send pictures, videos, food, letters, and whatever might make him laugh or put a smile on his face. The goal is graduation. Get him there. If his mind is shifted to that goal, his body will follow.

The Rest of Their Lives

Now is the time to relax and be confident that your teachings, your love, and your support have groomed your child to go out into the world and be productive. You can rest a little knowing that she will more than likely make the best decisions to enhance her life and the lives of the people around her. Once your child has finished college or trade school, found a place in the workforce, or launched a career in military, he's ready for complete independence, but he will always need your support or even your advice. He will decide where to build a life, who to marry or whether to marry at all, whether or not to have children and, if so, when to become a parent, and so many other things over which you will have little control. However, if you've done your job up until now, you can rest assured that he's likely to make good decisions most of the time.

As an adult, your child will also make mistakes in life, just as we still do as parents. Remember that he too is only human, and the best part of making mistakes is how he recovers from them. You've given the foundation to be able to recover well. Continue to be there for him, continue to love him, and because of what you've poured into him, he will be there for you as you age. It's a beautiful journey filled with beautiful memories. Enjoy it.

References

1. Planned Parenthood. (2016, March 10). How effective are condoms? Retrieved March 02, 2017, from https://www.plannedparenthood.org/learn/birth-control/condom/how-effective-are-condoms

2. CDC Fact Sheet: What Gay, Bisexual and Other Men Who Have Sex with Men Need to Know About Sexually Transmitted Diseases. (2016, October 18). Retrieved March 02, 2017, from https://www.cdc.gov/std/life-stages-populations/stdfact-msm.htm

3. The Office of Adolescent Health, U.S. Department of Health and Human Services." Office of Adolescent Health. N.p., 27 Feb. 2016. Web. 27 Feb. 2016. <http://www.hhs.gov/ash/oah/adolescent-health-topics/reproductive-health/teen-pregnancy/trends.html#>.

4. Pregnant Teen Mannequins at the Mall Are Sending a Mixed Message. (2014, November 13). Retrieved March 02, 2017, from https://www.yahoo.com/style/pregnant-teen-mannequins-at-the-mall-are-sending-a-102547296423.html

5. Folic acid: Why you need it before and during pregnancy | BabyCenter. (2013, March). Retrieved March 21, 2016, from http://www.babycenter.com/0_folic-acid-why-you-need-it-before-and-during-pregnancy_476.bc

6. The Dangers of Secondhand Smoke. (n.d.). Retrieved March 02, 2017, from https://www.healthychildren.org/English/health-issues/conditions/tobacco/Pages/Dangers-of-Secondhand-Smoke.aspx

7. Harding, D. M. (n.d.). Fetal Alcohol Syndrome. Alcohol in pregnancy and effects. Retrieved March 08, 2017, from http://paticnt.info/health/fetal-alcohol-syndrome-leaflet

8. Janitorial Cleaning Services. (n.d.). Retrieved November 28, 2016, from http://www.commercialofficecleaning.com/using-antibacterial-cleaning-products.html

9. Sudden infant death syndrome (SIDS) Causes. (n.d.). Retrieved March 02, 2017, from http://www.mayoclinic.org/diseases-conditions/sudden-infant-death-syndrome/basics/causes/CON-20020269

10. Gabriel, T. (2010, November 08). Proficiency of Black Students Is Found to Be Far Lower Than Expected. Retrieved March 02, 2017, from http://www.nytimes.com/2010/11/09/education/09gap.html'

11. Child Sexual Abuse Facts. (n.d.). Retrieved March 02, 2017, from http://www.cachouston.org/child-sexual-abuse-facts/

12. University of Texas Health Science Center at Houston. (2009, April 10). Middle School Youth As Young As 12 Engaging In Risky Sexual Activity. *ScienceDaily*. Retrieved March 14, 2017 from www.sciencedaily.com/releases/2009/04/090408145354.htm

13. HIV Among African Americans. (2017, February 22). Retrieved March 02, 2017, from https://www.cdc.gov/hiv/group/racialethnic/african americans/index.html

14. http://www.foxnews.com/health/2012/10/05/hidden-hormones-can-bring-about-early-puberty-in-kids.html

15. Merriam Webster https://www.merriam-webster.com

www.ingramcontent.com/pod-product-compliance
Lightning Source LLC
Chambersburg PA
CBHW031418290426
44110CB00011B/435